MARTY'S
WORLD FAMOUS™ COOKBOOK

Live, love, laugh.
My bad.
Marty.

MARTY'S

WORLD FAMOUS™ COOKBOOK

Secrets from the Muskoka
Landmark Café

Marty Curtis

Foreword by Chef Michael Smith

Photography by Douglas Bradshaw

whitecap

Edited by Lesley Cameron
Proofread by Joan E. Templeton
Design by Mauve Pagé and Robert Russell
Food photography by Douglas Bradshaw
Additional photography by Allan Dew, Paul Bennett,
    and Ryan Szulc
Food styling by Claire Stubbs

Printed in Canada by Friesens

**Library and Archives Canada Cataloguing
in Publication**

Curtis, Marty, 1970–
    Marty's world famous cookbook : secrets from the Muskoka
landmark café / Marty Curtis.

Includes index.
ISBN 978-1-55285-929-2

    1. Cookery. 2. Marty's World Famous Café. I. Title.

TX945.5.M37C87 2008   641.509713'16
C2008-900665-8

The publisher acknowledges the financial support of the
Government of Canada through the Book Publishing Industry
Development Program (BPIDP) and the Province of British
Columbia through the Book Publishing Tax Credit.

08 09 10 11 12 5 4 3 2 1

If you can, support your local food bank.

This book is dedicated to my mother, Heidi, for her creativity in the kitchen and unwavering support throughout the years. To my father, Martin, for his inventive mind and easy-going nature. To the memory of the late Honest Ed Mirvish who said, "Keep it simple, go against the trend, and fulfill a need." You were a mentor to me and to many others in Canada and around the world. You will be greatly missed. To Chris Haney, co-creator of Trivial Pursuit. Thank you for the opportunity of a lifetime and an education beyond university. To my late opa, thank you for teaching me strength and passion, and how to be a survivor. To people who help feed other people, you are humanitarians.

CONTENTS

FOREWORD

by Chef Michael Smith

This is a cookbook, not a "chefbook," because Marty Curtis is not a chef, he's a *cook*.

A chef wouldn't set out to make the very best buttertarts in the world, a chef would make fancy pastry with an unpronounceable name and hard-to-find ingredients. A chef wouldn't open a restaurant after toying with the idea of opening a shoe store, a chef would head for the big city and get lost on the way. And I'm not sure that a chef would always understand what Marty knows deep in his soul: food only comes alive when you share it. And I can tell you, anyone who's ever eaten his food is very, very thankful.

Marty's World Famous Café is not just a Muskoka landmark, it's a true icon of Canadian cuisine. It's the sort of place that feels like home the moment you walk in the door. It's filled with Marty's generous spirit and the spirit of all the staff, cottagers, fishermen, and guests who also call it home. It's not pretentious, it's real, and for food that tastes this good there is no higher compliment to give the cook—other than being inspired enough to make it yourself!

This is the sort of cookbook that will feel just right in your kitchen. It perfectly showcases the simple yet sophisticated flavours that easily empty plates and make a lot of work for Muskoka dishwashers. It highlights the real-world wisdom of Marty's kitchen. And it doesn't sound like a *chef* wrote it.

Frankly I can't believe Marty is giving up his secret buttertart recipe . . . However, I'm not that surprised—he's an extremely generous fellow. But seriously, this is bigger than Coke giving out their formula or Tim Hortons spilling their coffee bean secrets. I've personally tried out the recipe, and I'm pleased to report that now I can make the best buttertarts in the world too. And so can you. But neither of us will ever master the uniqueness that makes Marty's World Famous Café such a treasure.

Thanks for the buttertarts and thanks for the recipe, Marty!

Chef Michael Smith's car is about the same size
as one of Marty's world famous buttertarts.

ACKNOWLEDGEMENTS

I offer my heartfelt thanks to many people—

To **Chef Michael Smith**: you have given me many great words of wisdom, and your kind, generous nature has made a lasting impression. You're a great role model and a great human being. You're someone I look up to . . . literally. To **Doug Bradshaw** and **Claire Stubbs**: watching you two create great shot after great shot was a real treat for me and I enjoyed every moment. You guys really make great Buttertart Burgers. The Gladstone was a great choice **Lisette**, thank you. To **Janet Walkinshaw**: I love your choice of props. Thank you for making this book even better. We need you for book number two. To **Ryan Szulc**, **Dave Pidgeon**, and **David Grenier**: your behind-the-scenes efforts played a great role in the success of this book. Thank you all. When is Marty's T-shirt Day at the studio? I need a picture of that! To **Mario Batali**: thank you for sharing your pasta sauce recipe with me. Your passion for Italian cuisine is addictive and inspiring. Love the orange Crocs. To **Ted Reader**, Canada's grilling master, for adding to my fish-and-chips-night menu. Your Colonel Mustard's Slaw recipe is a hit. Plank you. To **Steven Raichlen**: your Chinese BBQ Sauce will have everyone licking their fingers. Thank you for sharing the recipe. I've learned so much from your books over the years and they continue to inspire me. To the people at CityTV, **Kevin Frankish and all his staff**: thank you for your generous support.

To Whitecap Publisher **Robert McCullough** for your faith in me, your knowledge, and your friendship. To all the **Whitecap staff** for their skills and for helping to turn my dream into a reality: thank you. To my other parents, **Marco and Jude**: you guys are perfect matches for my parents. Thank you for all your support over the years. To my brother **Austin** and sister **Aurora**: be happy, the future is bright. Love you both. To **Ursula, Honey, Ziggy, Inge**, and **Eddy**: the entrepreneurial spirit you all possess is highly admirable. To **Richard Brault**: thank you for your honesty, sincerity, and passion. Your product designs are fabulous and I am grateful for your advice and wisdom. The spirit of Richmond Street is alive. To **Wendy McCreary** of the NHL Alumni: thank you for your support and friendship. Your dad's hockey school taught me one thing . . . I should stick to food. To **Julie Van Rosendaal**: your words of advice, along with your kind nature and honesty, have shown me that you truly are "one smart cookie." To **Martin Kovnats**: thanks for helping me get this ball rolling. Your support and faith in me is something I will always cherish. To **Grant Cansfield**: thanks for your expert advice. Looking forward to a great future together. To the **staff at Marty's**: you have brought joy into the lives of many, and have given the gift of many happy memories. To **Tammy Goltz-Smellie** for helping with the proposal and manuscript. Your positive attitude is always a joy to experience. To **Hap Wilson**: thank you for the inspiration and earthly support. To **John Jones**: thank you for sharing your business knowledge and enthusiasm. Your advice has changed my life.

PREFACE

I wrote this book to share the legacy of the buttertart with every Canadian and everyone around the world who loves all things Canadian.

The buttertart is so much more than just a small pastry shell filled with brown sugar, butter, and eggs. It's a symbol of Canadiana and is proudly thought of as our national pastry. It's a tangible expression of the love and feeling the baker has for the people who will eat this creation. Buttertarts can bring joy and smiles. They have created—and will continue to create—great memories, emotion, and a sense of belonging.

Over the years Marty's has won several awards for its buttertarts. We're known throughout the world, and our customers come from too many countries to mention. It's now time for our secrets to be known to you, too, in recognition of your custom and loyalty. I'm honoured and delighted to be able to share my secret recipes with you and to do my part to preserve our Canadian National Pastry for future generations.

I feel genuinely privileged to be writing this book, sharing the passion and recipes that have brought me success with the public and my friends and family. For the record, *I am not a chef.* That is, I have no formal training, but I do have a genuine passion for cooking food that radiates love and I thoroughly enjoy sharing that food with as many people as I can. I've spent more than 20 years as a student of the world of food, exploring and creating recipes that taste great and are easy to make.

Marty's prides itself on bringing joy and a unique experience to local families, visitors, and cottagers here in Muskoka. We offer people a fun-filled time-out, and some welcome respite from the chaos and stresses of modern life. We aim to please with out-of-the-ordinary food: some healthy, some sinful, and some so good that people are left speechless.

I first tried to write this book eight years ago but I didn't get very far. Luckily for me, I later stumbled onto a Food Network television biography of Paula Deen. Her story motivated me so much I immediately started to draft this book, as I watched. I quickly realized that Paula and I had much in common. I too started with a low-budget enterprise: my main asset was my passion for serving quality food in a fun, friendly manner. I had an overwhelming sense that it was time to share with people how easy it can be to recreate these great-tasting recipes in your own home. (As I said, I am *not* a chef, so be assured that my methods are simple and easy to follow. Why make it complicated?) I had a fear of not knowing how to write this book, but once my heart was in the right place, the words seemed to flow much more easily from my pen to the page than they had ever done before.

I was fortunate to travel extensively at a young and impressionable age. My travel experiences taught me to "learn with my eyes" as my grandfather would say, and I quickly learned about people and their individual cultures, and our common reliance on food. Food is more than just fuel for the body. It fuels the spirit and holds us together as a community.

If there's one cookbook that becomes known as a true reflection of the soul of Canada, I hope it's this one.

Cook from the zone,
Marty

NHL legend Johnny Bower being served a Marty's Buttertart on a Curtis Curve Goalie Stick. "I'll take the other half home for my wife Nancy . . . She's the tart expert." He's one of the sweetest men you'll ever meet.

INTRODUCTION

LIVING THE DREAM

By the age of 14, I knew that one day I wanted to live on the water and own my own business. My parents and family members were all self-employed, so you could say that an entrepreneurial approach to life was in my blood.

At that time, I was working as a young apprentice at Baffo's Pizzeria and Restaurant, a fabulous pizzeria in Bolton, Ontario. Pizza-making was fun and creative, which resonated greatly with me. And on top of that, the atmosphere between the owners, Aldo and Charlie, and their staff felt friendly and secure. It was like working with family. I knew immediately that one day I would follow in Aldo and Charlie's footsteps and be an owner in the restaurant industry.

Working in the restaurant business throughout high school was financially rewarding. The after-school and weekend work paid off when I purchased my first car at the age of 15. That 1981 Mustang GL was so clean and polished, on a hot day you could have fried an egg and eaten it off the hood. I didn't have a licence, so I couldn't drive it but I sure could keep it looking good!

Then it came time to take my place at the University of Guelph's Business and Commerce Program. I had only one problem. I wasn't fond of school. I was more interested in getting out into the world and living my dream. I was tortured by the dilemma of whether to tough out four years of university or to let my family down. I was the first family member to attend university. I wasn't sure I also wanted to be the first to drop out.

My first two months of university had gone well from an academic perspective, but from a personal growth perspective, things weren't too good. I had to face the reality that I was bored. One afternoon, I was having lunch with Chris Haney, co-inventor of Trivial Pursuit, and he mentioned that travelling was the key to his success. He had learned a great deal from seeing the world, seeing new cultures, seeing how others live, and learning directly from people and their lifestyles. He was so convinced that travelling could help broaden my thinking and ultimately be a conduit to my success, that he offered me an opportunity to travel through Europe and Africa for a year, and to see many of the places, people, and things that he felt had contributed to his success.

I spent a restless night wondering how I was going to tell my family that I was quitting university to backpack around Europe. But one week later, I was somewhere over the Atlantic, headed first for Paris and then Berlin, where the Berlin Wall had come down just three weeks earlier. History was being made and I had to see it. I managed to chip off 10 pounds of the Berlin Wall, but I eventually gave most of it away to friends in Nerja, Spain, because my back and my backpack had had enough.

Every country in Europe had its own unique cuisine, drink, and social gatherings. I eagerly absorbed as much of the culture as I could, storing away memories of atmosphere and taste to be used in the next stage of my life journey. France, Germany, Austria, and Spain are just a few places where food, family, and friends made a lasting impression. But great memories were only a part of what I gained from my experience. It was character building and ultimately, life changing. I enjoyed the trip of a lifetime and gained a life education that no school could offer. I am forever grateful to Chris for making it possible. Perhaps the most important result of that year was that I learned a great deal about myself, and I started to understand who I was, what I valued, and what was important to me. It was a real eye-opener.

I returned home to Canada, brimming with energy and enthusiasm, and decided to bypass university in favour of following in my parents' footsteps into the real world of real estate. Aged 19 and green, I set out to knock the world on fire with my new-found wisdom and knowledge. And so I did. But after five years of successfully selling homes, it occurred to me that I was forever chasing money. Had I lost my true passion, the love of food? Where had my love of making people feel good gone? What had happened to the part of me that valued those things?

After a long debate with my inner voice, I left real estate and went to work for my grandfather in Orangeville, Ontario, where I learned about orthopaedic footwear. I soon realized that orthopaedic footwear truly made a difference in people's lives, and customers were genuinely grateful for our help. This job fulfilled my need to help others and gave me a certain inner peace that I had been missing.

One day, a good friend suggested I head for Bracebridge, Ontario, on my return home after a weekend visit to North Bay. I immediately saw an opportunity there to open my own orthopaedic footwear outlet. The Country Cobbler Shoe Store had closed its doors and the building was for sale. Only one problem . . . money. I had been successful in my real estate career but I had little left to show for it.

I considered renting out half the location to help supplement the mortgage payment. But who would I rent it to? What other business would do well in this location? I knew that Bracebridge is filled in the

(continued on page 20)

Being a true Canadian (born and raised), another of my passions—besides buttertarts—is my love for hockey. I, like many young Canadians across this country, dreamt of playing in the NHL. I grew up just north of Toronto in Bolton, Ontario, so I'm most passionate about the Toronto Maple Leafs. This passion for hockey probably got handed down from my dad, Martin Sr. In the early 1980s he invented and successfully patented the Curtis Curve Goalie Stick, which was approved by the NHL and first used by the great Glenn "Chico" Resch, and later by Andy Moog. (You can currently see it on display at the Hockey Hall of Fame in Toronto.)

In the summer of 2007, my friend Wendy McCreary asked me to participate at the annual NHL Alumni Charity Golf Tournament. This was a dream come true. Being surrounded by these hockey legends I had grown up watching and admiring is something I will never forget! But what became clear to me in short order was the true spirit of community, family, and compassion these players have. Their ongoing charity work left me inspired. Inspired to lend a hand to others when needed and to give to others without expecting anything in return . . .

Thank you all at the NHL Alumni. I'm glad you all loved the buttertarts.

The always handsome Ron Duguay

Legendary goaltender Johnny Bower

Fun and playful Dave Hutchinson

summer with tourists, cottagers, and people looking for fun with their families, and so the idea of ice cream came to mind. After a little more research and some meetings with friend and successful ice cream parlour owner, John Jones, I soon found myself drawn to this fun business instead of the world of orthopaedic footwear.

Driven by my irrepressible passion for food, I wrote an offer to purchase the vacant building with my remaining commission as the down payment and suggested a vendor take-back mortgage. To my surprise, the owner agreed to hold the mortgage and only wanted $10,000 more than my initial offer. For the first time in my 25 years, I had an opportunity to own real estate and my own business. Now all I needed was a business plan . . . or did I?

As best I could, I created a concept based on some wise words uttered by the late Honest Ed Mirvish in a CityTV interview some years earlier. When asked about the key to his success, he gladly replied, "Keep it simple, go against the trend, and fill a need." With these words in mind, after six weeks of preparation, I held the keys to the building and my new life. With no money left for renovations, I turned to friends and family for help. The most difficult parts of that first exciting month were washing in the Muskoka River and sleeping on the floor. Fortunately my time in Europe had prepared me well for unusual accommodations.

That first summer at Marty's World Famous Café was a success, but winter was fast approaching and I couldn't pay the mortgage with ice cream sales alone. I decided the time had come to take a chance and invested in a cappuccino machine, a pastry cooler, and an oven. Lunch, baked goods, and specialty coffees fused well with funky music and jam nights, and soon took Marty's to a whole new level. It also meant we survived the long Muskoka winters.

We became known for our use of premium ingredients, which helped establish our reputation as a quality place to eat. Soon enough, one by one, celebrity after celebrity started to visit and the Marty's Wall of Fame started to fill up. Marty's was a whole new concept for Bracebridge and we were seen as a unique entity in the town. I can honestly say that we've had customers from all over the world who've come in on the strength of our reputation.

I hope that one day you'll be one of those customers.

FINDING THE ZONE

The "zone" is the name I've given to the place deep inside our soul that harbours our ability to achieve anything we put our mind to. It's the place that refuses to be invaded by self-doubt, bad memories, lack of confidence, and other negative feelings. We all have our own zone, but it's not always easy to break through and unleash its potential. We need to work at finding ways into our zone. Once you've broken through, the rewards are incredible.

The simple exercises on the next two pages have guided me in my kitchen endeavours and other areas of my life. Be patient with yourself as you work through the exercises to find which of them, if any, work for you. Perseverance is key. Giving up won't get you anywhere. If none of these work for you, though, I hope they at least give you some inspiration to explore other methods. Find your zone!

BREATHE

Breathing is essential to life, but amazingly, many of us still aren't doing it properly. Breathing properly can help create calm and balance, two key ingredients to finding the zone. Before cooking, inhale deeply through your nose while expanding your stomach, hold your breath for a few seconds, then completely deflate your lungs. Focus on using your stomach to exhale slowly, releasing more air than you've taken in. Try this three or four times before you begin cooking. This exercise will relax you both physiologically and psychologically.

VISUALIZE

Next, visualize the finished dish before you begin. This will dramatically increase your chances of success. It's important to see, and even more important that you feel, the end results because that's how they will manifest. Picture yourself adding the ingredients with your hands working through the process; imagine the smell of the dish you are creating and feel the perfect end result. You can be the master of visualization in your own kitchen. Go ahead, give it a try. No one's watching. "Imagination is everything. It is the preview of life's coming attractions." The quote is from Albert Einstein. I think he knew what he was talking about.

LET IT GO

After breathing and visualizing, you then need to trust yourself and nurture a feeling of "knowing," a gut feeling that tells you: you can do this. Once you feel that sense of knowing, you'll feel a difference. You can then begin. You will succeed.

BE CONFIDENT

Confidence is everything. Having confidence in yourself will produce the results you're looking for. "Whether you think you can or you can't, either way you are right." (Henry Ford [1863–1947])

BE ORGANIZED

Read every recipe thoroughly until you can "feel" it coming together. This will help kick-start the visual process, and positive thoughts of success will bring you confidence. Have all your ingredients set in front of you before you begin to prepare any recipe or meal. These two simple steps eliminate the frustration of discovering you're short of a particular ingredient, and keep you in the zone.

PLAY MUSIC

Music is an amazing tool than can help establish your zone. I like to listen to something that reflects how I'm feeling. It can take cooking to a whole new level. Cooking is supposed to be fun, and when it is, you'll see it reflected in your finished dish. While I was writing this book, I thoroughly enjoyed the sounds of Jack Johnson's album *In Between Dreams*. Give it a listen. It's fantastic.

PAY ATTENTION TO THE LIGHTING

Set the mood. Light some candles, dim the lights, or open the blinds, whatever's appropriate. I've always enjoyed the mood created by track lighting in my kitchens. It's warm and cozy and quite simply, it feels good.

HAVE A DRINK

Enjoy a glass of wine, a cold beer, or your favourite cocktail. This is supposed to be fun. Or have a soda or a great cup of coffee—whatever you enjoy.

LIGHT A FIRE

Muskoka winters can be tremendously cold and so this really works for me. The warmth of a fireplace gives off radiant heat. It warms objects in the room instead of heating the air. That's why it feels good.

When all else fails . . . pray!

MUSKOKA MORNINGS

Muskoka mornings are truly magical. The water is calm, the birds are singing in the trees, and loon calls echo across the lake as the mist rises and the sun breaks the horizon.

The air is fresh and clean. What a perfect setting for the most important meal of the day.

COFFEE HOUSE SECRETS

What better way to start the day than with a great cup of coffee? Here's how.

THE BEST BEANS MAKE THE BEST COFFEE

Our roaster, Reunion Island, is known for exceptional coffee beans, and owner Peter Pesce is said to be the best cupper in Canada. His palate is a legend in its own lifetime. To say that Peter is fussy about quality is a supreme example of understatement.

FILTERED WATER

Muskoka's natural water supply is fantastic, but we do filter it before using it to brew. Use natural spring water at home if you possibly can.

BUY WHOLE BEANS IN SMALL AMOUNTS

Buying smaller quantities of beans will help stop them from going stale. Coffee beans have properties like those of peanuts and can absorb moisture if exposed to air, but I think of coffee beans like I do a loaf of bread. Keep them in an airtight container at room temperature and consume quickly for maximum freshness. Please do not freeze your beans. Freezing causes them to absorb moisture and the aromas of other foods in the freezer, both of which will destroy the natural flavour of the beans.

ALWAYS GRIND FRESH

Grinding beans fresh releases their full flavour and full potential. If you buy good-quality beans you may find that a weaker bean can produce a fuller flavour, when finely ground. However, be aware that if you fine-grind a full-flavoured bean, your coffee may have a muddy or mucky flavour.

HOW MUCH COFFEE SHOULD I USE?

I prefer a flavourful cup of coffee, which requires heavier ounceage. At the café we use 2¼–2¾ oz for a 10-cup pot, depending on the variety. The proper ounceage should produce a full-flavoured, but not bitter, coffee.

HOW TO MAKE SPECIALTY COFFEE

Our most sought-after specialty drinks are cappuccinos and lattes. We've made a few over the years. If I had a dollar for every . . . never mind.

THE GOLDEN RULE

Always begin with a cold jug and cold milk. After steaming the milk, let it cool. This allows the bubbles in the milk to set, which will create perfectly sculpted foam. Homogenized milk makes the greatest flavour with a softer foam, 2% milk makes better foam with adequate flavour, and skim milk makes the hardest foam with the least amount of flavour. Play with it until you know what you prefer.

THE JUG MEETS THE WAND

Fill your cold frothing jug one-third full of the cold milk of your choice. Submerge the steam wand into the milk and hold on a slight angle. Turn on the steam. Keep the head of the steam wand just at the surface, half in and half out, creating a squelching noise. Focus on the wand sitting half in and half out at all times, lowering the jug as the milk expands. When your milk reaches 160°F, you're done (use a clip-on thermometer in your frothing jug for optimum accuracy). Set the jug aside and tamp on the counter to harden and condense the air bubbles for better foam.

All specialty coffee drinks are made with espresso, milk, and foam; it's the ratio of ingredients that change the flavour and the name of the coffee.

THE PERFECT ESPRESSO SHOT

When the right espresso bean is ground perfectly, portioned correctly, and filled into a hot brew handle, then tamped with the right pressure, and poured into a warm cup creating a rich creamy swirled tiger-stripe pattern, then and only then has a perfect espresso been poured. Espresso is the base for several other types of coffees.

Cappuccino
⅓ espresso
⅓ steamed milk
⅓ foam
Top with cocoa, cinnamon, or shaved chocolate.

Latte
⅓ espresso
⅔ steamed milk
Top the thin layer of foam with cocoa, cinnamon, or shaved chocolate.

Muskoka Mocha
⅓ espresso
⅔ steamed hot chocolate (milk and chocolate sauce)
Top the thin layer of foam with real whipped cream and shaved chocolate or cocoa powder.

Café au Lait
⅓ espresso topped to halfway with hot water or ½ cup traditionally brewed dark French roast coffee
½ cup steamed milk
This gives a thin layer of foam.

Café Confidential: Try any of these drinks with an ounce of maple syrup or Baileys Irish Cream.

THE FLUFFIEST OMELETTE EVER

When I first started making omelettes as a kid, I would brown them too much. Since I prefer a softer texture, I learned this trick from watching programs on the Food Network. I can now produce a perfect omelette. Try it. Serves 2

3 Tbsp butter
¼ cup minced onion
¼ cup minced red bell pepper
4 eggs
½ cup 10% cream
½ tsp dried mustard powder
pinch nutmeg

kosher salt and freshly ground
    black pepper to taste
¼ cup chopped ham (optional)
¼ cup sliced mushrooms (optional)
¼ cup shredded cheddar cheese
    (optional)

Preheat oven to 350°F.

Over medium-low heat, in a non-stick ovenproof skillet, melt the butter and sauté the onion and red pepper for about 5 minutes.

In a bowl, whisk together the eggs, cream, dried mustard powder, nutmeg, and salt and pepper. Add this to the skillet. Cook for about 1 minute gently scraping the sides toward the middle with a heatproof spatula. (This will resemble the early stages of making scrambled eggs.) Add your optional ingredients now.

Place in the oven for 3–5 minutes or just until the egg is firm. Serve, creating a French fold: first fold the omelette by one-third in the pan using a spatula, then tip it over onto a plate creating the second fold.

Café Confidential: Play with your filling options:
- Cheese: brie, Swiss, Beemster, Stilton
- Veggies: asparagus, green bell pepper, broccoli, mushrooms
- Meat: cooked sausage pieces, black forest ham, prosciutto, cooked back bacon, maple bacon

PICK A PANCAKE

Great breakfasts can create lifelong memories. If you've ever been woken up by the smell of pancakes, you should enjoy these proven pancake winners, all of which were tested and joyfully eaten. Start with the fluffy pancake base and create from there. Serves 4

2 cups all-purpose flour
2 Tbsp baking powder
½ tsp kosher salt

2 eggs
2 cups 2% milk
6 Tbsp peanut oil, divided

In a bowl, whisk together the flour, baking powder, and salt, and then add the eggs, milk, and 2 Tbsp of the oil, and whisk to remove any lumps. Preheat a large skillet, and add enough oil to coat the surface. Hot oil is the key to great pancakes. When a drop of water spatters in the pan, pour away. When bubbles form on top of the batter and the bottom is browned, about 3–4 minutes, flip and cook for another 2–3 minutes. Remove from the pan, and serve topped with a pat of butter and pure maple syrup. Try adding raspberry or strawberry jam on top of that. It's delicious.

Café Confidential: I prefer to cook my pancake in small amounts of peanut oil rather than butter, as butter sometimes burns. The oil makes the perfect brown-crusted rim around the outer edge of the pancake. I end up using about 4 Tbsp per recipe.

Be creative. Add any of these ingredients to the batter, or mix and match to create a flavour all your own:

APPLE JACK
1 large apple, peeled, cored,
    and shredded
1 tsp cinnamon
½ cup raisins (optional)
½ cup walnuts, pieces (optional)

LEMON, RASPBERRY,
AND CREAM CHEESE
1 cup raspberries
¾ cup cream cheese, cut into
    pea-sized bits
1–2 Tbsp lemon rind

BANANA CHOCOLATE CHIP
1 diced banana
½ cup chocolate chips

CRANBERRY ORANGE
½ cup dried cranberries
rind and juice of 1 orange

MUSKOKA BERRY
¼ cup fresh blueberries
¼ cup fresh raspberries
¼ cup fresh blackberries

EGGS BENEDICT WITH MELTED BRIE AND ASPARAGUS

This is without a doubt my all-time favourite Sunday breakfast treat. Topped with a thin slice of brie then quickly broiled, this twist on a classic is worth trying. Serves 2–4

½ cup unsalted butter
½ tsp white vinegar
3 egg yolks
1½ Tbsp lemon juice
kosher salt and freshly ground
    black pepper to taste

8 asparagus spears
4 slices smoked breakfast ham
4 eggs
2 English muffins, halved
4 slices of brie

Begin by making the clarified butter. In a small saucepan over medium heat, melt the butter completely and carefully pour into a measuring cup, leaving behind the cloudy "buttermilk" at the bottom of the saucepan. The liquid in the measuring cup is now clarified butter.

Fill a saucepan three-quarters full with water, add the ½ tsp vinegar, and place over medium heat. This is for the poached eggs. The water is ready when champagne-like bubbles appear.

Meanwhile, prepare the hollandaise sauce. In a double boiler over low heat, whisk the egg yolks and slowly add the clarified butter in a slow stream. Whisk gently so the egg yolk and butter form a rich, thick sauce. At this stage add the lemon juice and salt and pepper to taste, and continue to whisk. Remove from the heat to prevent the sauce from cooking or curdling.

In a steamer, steam the asparagus and ham together until tender, 4–5 minutes.

Meanwhile, poach the eggs in the simmering water until the centres start to jell, 3–4 minutes. Toast the English muffins. Preheat broiler to high. Place a toasted English muffin in the centre of a plate. Add a dollop of hollandaise sauce, layer on a slice of ham, 2 asparagus spears, and an egg, and top with 2 slices of the brie. Broil for 1 minute or just until the brie starts to melt. Remove and top with more hollandaise sauce. Serve with a smile.

Café Confidential: To perfect the timing for this recipe, read it through carefully and visualize the process in your mind. When you can see the process, begin. For a vegetarian version, replace the ham with sautéed mushrooms. It's fantastic.

SUNDAY MORNING HASH BROWNS

Waking up to the incredible aroma of Mom cooking bacon and onions was a sure sign that it was Sunday morning in our household. A few leftover potatoes from Saturday night's dinner became this Sunday morning classic that's forever ingrained in my memory. Serve with eggs and bacon, or use as a substitute for the English muffins in Eggs Benedict with Melted Brie and Asparagus (page 32). Serves 4

2 strips bacon, chopped
½ cup finely chopped onion
4 cups shredded cooked potatoes

kosher salt and freshly ground
black pepper to taste
¾ cup peanut oil

In a small saucepan over medium heat, cook the chopped bacon for 3 minutes. Add the onion and stir. Cook just until the onion softens, 3–5 minutes. In a bowl, place the bacon, onion, shredded potato, and salt and pepper to taste, and fold to combine.

Heat the peanut oil in a large skillet over medium heat. Form the potato mixture into 4 equal patties and place carefully in the hot oil. Cook about 10 minutes per side or until evenly browned but not burnt. Serve.

BREAKFAST IN A PAN

This recipe was introduced to me by the Houle family one Christmas morning in Hamilton, Ontario. It was prepared on Christmas Eve and the smell of this concoction, spreading its magical aroma throughout the house on Christmas morning, was something I'll never forget. Simple and delicious. Serves 6–8

6 eggs
2 cups 10% cream
1 cup 2% milk
½ cup minced onion
½ cup minced red onion
2 tsp dried mustard powder
2 tsp Worcestershire sauce
½ tsp kosher salt

½ tsp freshly ground black pepper
dash Tabasco sauce
1 loaf sliced bread (whole-grain or white, whichever you prefer)
8 slices cheddar cheese
8–10 slices black forest ham
⅓ cup melted butter
4–6 cups cereal

Grease the bottom and sides of a Marty's Big Ass Pan (see page 159) or 9- × 13-inch deep-dish ovenproof pan.

In a bowl mix together the eggs, cream, milk, both onions, dried mustard powder, Worcestershire sauce, salt, pepper, and Tabasco sauce. Set aside.

Layer the bottom of the prepared pan with 4–5 slices of the bread, avoiding overlapping. Pour one-third of the egg mixture over the bread. Add 4 slices of the cheddar cheese and 4–5 slices of the ham. Then add another layer of bread. Pour another one-third of the egg mixture over the bread. Add another 4 slices of cheddar and 4–5 slices of ham. Finish with 4 slices of bread and the remaining egg mixture poured overtop. Cover and refrigerate overnight.

In the morning, preheat oven to 350°F.

Pour ⅓ cup melted butter over the egg dish and sprinkle with your favourite breakfast cereal.

Bake for 60–70 minutes. Slice and serve.

SMOOTHIES

These recipes were created when I was playing around with a commercial juicer. A blender works perfectly for this great breakfast starter. Here are seven ways with smoothies. Makes two 8 oz glasses, unless otherwise noted

FAT-BURNER SMOOTHIE

½ cup fresh pineapple chunks
½ cup ice cubes
½ grapefruit, peeled, seeded,
    and chopped
3 large strawberries
¼ cup carrot juice

Combine all the ingredients in a blender until smooth.

BANANA SPLIT SMOOTHIE

This is a fun and easy way for kids to eat their fruits.

1 banana, peeled and cut
    into chunks
3 large strawberries
½ cup fresh pineapple chunks
½ cup ice cubes
½ cup 2% milk

Combine all the ingredients in a blender until smooth.

ANTIOXIDANT SMOOTHIE

½ cup blueberries or POM juice
    (pomegranate)
½ cup raspberries
½ cup cranberry juice
½ cup ice cubes

Combine all the ingredients in a blender until smooth.

MORNING GLORY SMOOTHIE

1 banana, peeled and cut
    into chunks
½ cup fresh pineapple chunks
½ cup grapes
½ cup carrot juice
½ cup ice cubes

Combine all the ingredients in a blender until smooth.

CHOCOLATE PROTEIN SHAKE

1 cup soy milk
1 cup ice cubes
2 Tbsp whey protein powder,
   chocolate flavour
2 Tbsp chocolate syrup (optional)

Combine all the ingredients
in a blender until smooth.

MUSKOKA SMOOTHIE

1 cup ice cubes
¾ cup 2% milk
½ cup wild blueberries
½ cup fresh raspberries
1 Tbsp maple syrup

Combine all the ingredients
in a blender until smooth.

ORANGE SMOOTHIE
Makes four 8 oz glasses

1½ cups freshly squeezed
   orange juice
1½ cups ice cubes
¾ cup water
3 egg whites
¼ cup granulated sugar
1 tsp vanilla

Combine all the ingredients except
the ice in a blender until sugar
dissolves, about 30 seconds.
Add the ice and blend 30 seconds.

Café Confidential: Save the egg yolks
for the hollandaise sauce portion of the
Eggs Benedict with Melted Brie and
Asparagus recipe (page 32).

LEMON, BLUEBERRY, AND CREAM CHEESE MUFFINS

There's often a lineup for these one-of-a-kind muffins. They're easy to make, too. You can substitute the blueberries with equal amounts of raspberries, strawberries, or blackberries for an entirely new muffin experience.
Makes 6 jumbo muffins

MUFFINS
2½ cups all-purpose flour
1⅓ cups granulated sugar
3 tsp baking powder
one 8 oz package low-fat cream cheese
2 eggs
⅔ cup vegetable oil
1 cup 2% milk

¼ cup freshly squeezed lemon juice
1–2 Tbsp lemon rind
1 cup frozen blueberries

GLAZE
1½ cups icing sugar
¼ cup lemon juice
1 Tbsp lemon rind

Preheat oven to 375°F. Grease a 6-cup jumbo muffin pan (see page 159) or Marty's Buttertart Pan (see page 150).

For the muffins, whisk together the flour, sugar, and baking powder in a bowl.

Warm a knife in hot water, cut the cream cheese into julienne strips, and then cross-cut into pea-sized bits. Warm the knife regularly for smooth cuts. Add cream cheese to the dry ingredients. Break up the bits by stirring with the head of a whisk.

In another bowl, whisk the eggs, then whisk in the oil, then the milk and lemon juice and rind. Add to the dry ingredients and fold until just combined.

Add the blueberries, and fold gently.

Fill the prepared pan with batter to just under the top line. Bake for 30–35 minutes.

Cool in the pan for 30 minutes. Meanwhile, make the glaze by combining the icing sugar with the lemon juice and rind. Add a touch of hot water if the glaze needs to be thinner. Brush over the muffins.

BANANA NUT BREAD

How can anyone resist the temptation of a fresh piece of warm banana bread with a smidge of butter? This recipe is easy to make, and if there's any left over it makes a great snack in the kids' lunches. Make sure all the ingredients are at room temperature. Makes one 9- × 5-inch loaf

1⅔ cups all-purpose flour
1 tsp kosher salt
½ tsp baking soda
½ tsp baking powder
6 Tbsp butter
¾ cup granulated sugar
3 eggs

2 bananas, very ripe, about
1 cup mashed
¾ cup walnut pieces

GLAZE (OPTIONAL)
1 cup icing sugar
½ cup melted butter

Preheat oven to 350°F. Grease a 9- × 5-inch loaf pan.

In a medium-sized bowl, whisk together the flour, salt, baking soda, and baking powder. Set aside. In another bowl with a hand-held electric mixer, blend the butter and sugar until light and fluffy, about 3 minutes. Slowly add the flour mixture to the butter mixture until it resembles granular brown sugar. Add the eggs one at a time, mixing well, until just combined.

Use a spatula to fold in the banana and nuts until just combined. Pour into the prepared pan.

Bake for 50–60 minutes or until a cake tester inserted in the centre comes out clean.

This can be eaten without the glaze, but it does add a certain something!

For the glaze, in a bowl add the ½ cup of melted butter into the icing sugar. Whisk until blended and brush over the top of the loaf. Let cool in the pan, remove from the pan, and cut into slices.

CRANBERRY ORANGE LOAF

Bala, Ontario, is located on Highway 118 on the west side of Lake Muskoka, and is one of North America's largest cranberry-producing regions. Inspired by Johnston's Cranberry Farm in Bala, this recipe is ideal for late fall or Christmas time. Serve this warm with a smidge of butter. Life is good.
Makes a 9- × 5-inch loaf

LOAF
2 cups all-purpose flour
2 Tbsp orange rind
1½ tsp baking powder
½ tsp baking soda
½ tsp kosher salt
1½ cups fresh cranberries
½ cup pecans, pieces
¼ cup unsalted butter

1 cup granulated sugar
1 egg
½ cup freshly squeezed orange juice
   (about 1 big orange)

GLAZE
⅔ cup icing sugar
rind and juice of 1 orange

Preheat oven to 350°F. Grease a 9- × 5-inch loaf pan.

In a bowl whisk together the flour, orange rind, baking powder, baking soda, and salt. Stir in the cranberries and pecans. Set aside.

In a large clean bowl, cream together the butter, sugar, and egg. Stir in the orange juice. Add the flour mixture and stir until just combined. Pour into the prepared loaf pan. Bake for 1 hour or until toothpick inserted in the centre comes out clean.

For the glaze, combine the icing sugar, rind, and juice. Brush over the loaf while still warm in the pan to allow the glaze to soak in. Cool in the pan for 1 hour, cut, and serve.

SOUP OR SALAD?

Soup comforts the soul and salad energizes it. Is there any wonder they're on almost every menu in the world? These recipes are delicious and fun to make at the same time, and they get great reviews. Enjoy.

When we work together we can create something to be proud of.

STONE SOUP

You may already be familiar with the legend, or a variation on the legend, of the stone soup. Some have interpreted this story as a warning against strangers who bring little and take away much. Others, like me, think of this story as an example of co-operation and an illustration of how food brings us together as a community. When we start with practically nothing, it takes only a little help from others to produce a significant something. When we work together we can create something to be proud of.

Different versions of this story are set all around the world, but Portuguese tradition insists that stone soup was created in Almeirim, Portugal, and many restaurants in that city list their own version of **sopa de pedra** (stone soup) on their menu.

There was once a group of travellers, weary from many weeks of walking and hungry from lack of food. They came to a village nestled in a forest and settled down to pass the night there. One of the travellers asked the villagers if there was any food to spare, but his efforts were rebuffed and he returned empty-handed to his companions. Unfazed by the reaction of the villagers, the travellers settled down in front of a campfire on which they placed a small pot filled with water. As the water heated, one of the travellers placed a stone in the bottom of the pot. Some of the villagers had been watching the travellers from behind a tree. Emboldened by curiosity, they came out from their hiding place and asked the travellers why they had placed a stone in the pot. "Why, we are making stone soup, of course," replied one of the travellers. "Would you care to share some with us? All it needs now is a little garnish. Perhaps you could help?" The villagers, reluctant to share too much of their food but anxious to taste this strange concoction, each went off to their homes in search of something small to add to the pot. Soon the water was warming a fine selection of vegetables as well as the stone, and the travellers and villagers enjoyed their tasty, nourishing soup together.

SOUL FOR THE CHICKEN SOUP

Many times a week at Marty's my hands will pick apart a roasted chicken, and every once in a while I find myself thanking the chicken for its sacrifice. I make sure to use every morsel of meat and I even boil the carcass for chicken stock (page 55). This soup is a tribute to the bird that we often take for granted. Is it any wonder this soup makes us feel better when we are under the weather? Feed your soul. Serves 16

2 Tbsp olive oil
2 carrots, chopped
2 celery stalks, chopped
1 leek or onion, chopped
kosher salt and freshly ground black
    pepper to taste
2½ cups water

3½ quarts chicken stock
    (page 55)
2 cups cooked and chopped
    chicken meat
½ cup chopped fresh parsley
½ tsp garlic powder
1 bay leaf

Heat the olive oil in a large stockpot over medium-high heat. Add the carrots, celery, leek, and salt and pepper to taste. Brown for 10 minutes, then deglaze with ½ cup of the water and stir. Add all the remaining ingredients and bring to a gentle boil. Reduce the heat to low, cover, and simmer until the vegetables are tender. Season to taste with more salt and pepper.

Café Confidential: Try a hint of thyme and rosemary for some extra zing. Or add ½ cup of uncooked rice or pasta, for a more substantial soup. Have fun with it.

MARTY'S RED PEPPER SOUP

People frequently comment that this is the best soup they've ever had. When they ask what kind it is, I always smile and say "Campbell's." It looks like the secret's well and truly out. This is a twist on the classic Campbell's Tomato Soup. You'll love it. Serves 8

¾ cup olive oil

7 garlic cloves, crushed

1 large ripe red bell pepper, diced fine

½ red onion, diced fine

1 tsp kosher salt

½ tsp freshly ground black pepper

3 Tbsp dried basil

1 cup red wine

five 10 oz cans Campbell's Tomato Soup

50 oz 2% milk (use the soup can to measure as per can instructions)

5–6 Tbsp granulated sugar

Our Best Croutons (page 58)

Garlic Drizzle (page 56)

Heat the oil in a large pot over medium-high heat. Add the garlic, red pepper, onion, salt, and pepper. Brown and let stick to the bottom and caramelize, about 10 minutes. Stir to lift the veggies from the bottom of the pot. Add the basil and let stick again, 4–5 minutes. Deglaze with the red wine and cook for 3–5 minutes.

Add the tomato soup and milk, and stir. Add the sugar. Bring to a boil while whisking to prevent sticking. Reduce the heat to low, cover, and simmer for half an hour. Serve with Our Best Croutons and a few drops of Garlic Drizzle. This soup improves the longer it simmers.

HEIDI'S BEETLESS BORSCHT

This slow-cooking veggie stew is my mom's favourite. It gives her the opportunity to clean out her fridge and make the house smell great at the same time. This meal in a bowl doesn't last long when we serve it at the café. Serves 10–14

3 Tbsp olive oil

2 smoked pork chops (or 1 smoked pork hock or 2 smoked sausages or ½ rack smoked ribs)

3 medium onions, chopped

4 cloves garlic, chopped

12 cups water or chicken stock (page 55)

6 whole tomatoes, diced

3 potatoes, peeled and cubed

2 cups cauliflower florets

2 cups chopped green beans, 1-inch pieces

2 cups ketchup (the secret ingredient!)

3 carrots, peeled and sliced

3 celery stalks, chopped

½ medium cabbage, shredded

½ medium turnip, peeled and cubed

1–2 bouillon cubes

2 bay leaves

¼ cup chopped fresh parsley

kosher salt and freshly ground black pepper to taste

In a skillet over medium heat, add 1 Tbsp of the olive oil and heat. Add the pork chops, fry for 5 minutes per side, and set aside.

In a large soup pot over medium heat, add the remaining 2 Tbsp olive oil, onions, and garlic and sweat for 5 minutes. Add the remaining ingredients except the parsley and salt and pepper and stir. Cut the pork chops into small chunks and add to the pot. Bring to a boil. Reduce the heat to low and simmer, covered, for 2–3 hours. Add the parsley and season to taste with the salt and pepper.

Patience is a real virtue when making this dish as the flavours need time to develop to their full potential.

Serve with a dollop of sour cream.

Café Confidential: The secret ingredient: ketchup. The vinegar and sugar combined with the tomato lend themselves well to the overall flavour.

OPA'S MUSHROOM SOUP

This incredible soup is a tribute to my late opa, Ziggy. Among his many passions were Sunday drives with my oma, Elizabeth. They would often drive for miles in search of wild mushrooms. Many times we would get the call, "We're in Banff . . . we found them . . . don't know when we'll be back." Here's to you, Opa. Serves 4–6

4 Tbsp olive oil

3 Tbsp butter

2 lb cremini mushrooms, sliced

¾ cup chopped shallots

1 clove garlic, chopped

¾ tsp kosher salt

½ tsp freshly ground black pepper

4 Tbsp sherry or white wine

6 Tbsp all-purpose flour

2 Tbsp fresh thyme

5 cups warm chicken stock (page 55)

½ cup whipping cream (35%)

2–3 Tbsp fresh parsley

Our Best Croutons (page 58)

Garlic Drizzle (page 56)

In a large saucepan over medium-high heat, heat the olive oil and butter, and sauté the mushrooms, shallots, garlic, salt, and pepper for 5 minutes or until mushrooms soften.

Add the sherry and stir. Cook for 2 minutes. Reduce the heat and add the flour and thyme, stirring with a whisk. Add the chicken stock and stir until smooth. Add the cream and return to high heat, stirring constantly.

As the soup thickens and approaches the boiling point, lower the heat to return to a simmer. Add the fresh parsley and stir. Garnish with Our Best Croutons and a touch of Garlic Drizzle.

OLD ENGLISH LEEK AND POTATO SOUP

This soup reminds me of England and many Sunday visits to the countryside. For only a few pounds you can tuck up by the fireside in an English country inn and enjoy a pint, a cheese and onion sandwich, and a piping-hot bowl of leek and potato soup. What a fun way to experience England on a cold, drizzly Sunday afternoon. Makes about 12 cups

6 bacon strips, chopped small
3 Tbsp butter
8 leeks, cleaned and chopped
¼ cup water
3 baking potatoes, cubed
6 cups chicken stock (page 55)
½ cup 10% cream
¾ tsp kosher salt
½ tsp freshly ground black pepper
chives, chopped for garnish
Garlic Drizzle (page 56)

In a large stockpot over medium heat, crisp the bacon. Set aside.

Add 1 Tbsp of the butter to the bacon drippings. Add the leeks and water. Cook, stirring for 15 minutes. Add the potatoes and chicken stock and bring to a boil. Reduce the heat and simmer, covered, for 1 hour. Add the remaining 2 Tbsp of butter, cream, and salt and pepper; cook and stir 5 minutes more. Cool, then purée until smooth.

Serve with the reserved bacon bits, chives, and few drops of Garlic Drizzle.

Café Confidential: *Kosher Salt versus Iodized Salt*
I once attended a seminar where Chef Michael Smith was demonstrating the difference between taste and flavour. He also explained the four basic taste sensations: sweet, salty, spicy, and sour. He gave everyone a chance to test out the difference between the four.

You can try it yourself. Take a lemon wedge and rub the rind against your teeth. What is the flavour? Lemon. Now bite the lemon and what is the taste sensation? Sourness. We also tested the difference between kosher and iodized salt. I urge you to taste the difference for yourself. Kosher salt has a natural flavour and iodized salt has a chemical-like flavour. Use kosher whenever you can.

CURRIED SQUASH AND GINGER SOUP

This soup can only be described as delicious. Its body and flavour are so special, I recommend you try this recipe at least once. Serves 14–16

1 hubbard squash (use an 8 lb squash or enough to make 6 cups cooked)
½ cup brown sugar, packed
½ cup butter, chilled and chopped
kosher salt and freshly ground black pepper to taste
1 leek, white part only, chopped

½ red onion, chopped
7 cups chicken stock (page 55)
1 Tbsp powdered ginger
1 Tbsp curry powder
1 tsp kosher salt
½ tsp freshly ground black pepper

Preheat oven to 350°F.

Cut the hubbard squash in half lengthwise. Scoop out and discard the seeds and loose strands of flesh. Sprinkle both halves of the squash evenly with the brown sugar. Add ¼ cup of the butter to the cavity of each half. Sprinkle with salt and pepper to taste. Bake, uncovered, for 1–1½ hours, until fork-tender. Remove from the oven and let cool. Pour off the butter and brown sugar from the centre of the squash and set aside. Remove the flesh, set it aside, and discard the skin.

Over medium heat in a large stockpot, add the reserved butter liquid. Add the leek and onion and sauté for 10 minutes. Add 2 cups of the chicken stock, powdered ginger, curry powder, salt, and pepper, bring to a slow boil, and cook for 10 minutes more. Add the squash and the remaining 5 cups of chicken stock and bring to a boil. Reduce the heat and simmer, covered, 1–1½ hours, stirring occasionally. Cool, purée, reheat, and serve.

Café Confidential: Try adding a pinch of nutmeg or ½ cup coconut milk with the 2 cups of chicken stock. Enjoy.

CHICKEN STOCK

Creating a good stock is a simple yet rewarding process. This will add depth of flavour in soups, stews, and rice dishes such as paella. And it comes with a bonus: the aroma alone from this recipe will trigger comforting memories of home. Makes 8–10 cups

2 Tbsp olive oil
4 cloves garlic, chopped
2 carrots, chopped
2 celery stalks, chopped
1 onion, diced

1–2 chicken carcasses (bones only of whole cooked chicken)
1–2 bouillon cubes, chicken flavour
1 bay leaf
kosher salt and freshly ground black pepper to taste

In a large stockpot over medium heat, add the olive oil, garlic, carrots, celery, and onion and sweat for 5 minutes. Add all the chicken bones. Add enough water to cover completely, 1 bouillon cube, and the bay leaf. Bring to a boil. Reduce the heat and simmer, covered, for 1 hour.

Taste the stock and season to taste. For a stronger chicken flavour, add the second bouillon cube. Simmer, covered, for another hour. Add more salt and pepper to taste.

Remove from the heat, strain, and refrigerate. Once cooled, remove the fat from the top.

Café Confidential: This stock also works well when made with any leftover turkey from Thanksgiving dinner instead of chicken. The turkey version is excellent in Big Ass Turkey Pie (page 183).

GARLIC DRIZZLE

STORE SECRET

This is an indispensable secret ingredient accent for all manner of dishes from soups and salads to pizzas and wraps. People really notice the aroma of fresh garlic, and their eating experience begins with a bang. You'll find this in a number of recipes in this book. Makes 1 cup

1 cup extra virgin olive oil   7 fresh garlic cloves, crushed

Combine well in an airtight jar. Refrigerate for up to 15 days.

Café Confidential: Don't underestimate the importance of a dish's aroma. A tempting aroma can stimulate your appetite and even make food seem to taste better. If our sense of smell is impaired, foods taste bland. Interestingly, though, we can still distinguish between salty and sweet tastes.

Café Confidential: *Easy-Peel Garlic*
Separate the cloves from the bud, smash them with the side of a chef's knife, and peel with wet hands. The peel sticks to the water on your hands.

MARTY'S KILLER CAESAR SALAD

This is my favourite salad to make and it receives many, many compliments from our customers. Fresh dressing, flavourful croutons, and real Parmesan combined with bacon chunks and Garlic Drizzle put this salad ahead of the rest. It's definitely worth a try. Serves 4

DRESSING

10 anchovy fillets

4–5 garlic cloves

2 eggs yolks

¼ cup red wine vinegar or freshly
    squeezed lemon juice

2 Tbsp Dijon mustard

3 dashes of Worcestershire sauce

1 tsp kosher salt or to taste

½ tsp freshly ground black pepper
    or to taste

1 cup olive oil

SALAD

1 head romaine lettuce, washed and dried

salt and freshly ground black pepper
    to taste

2–3 Tbsp Garlic Drizzle (page 56)

2 cups Our Best Croutons (page 58)

4–6 bacon strips, baked crisp and
    chopped into ½-inch chunks

¼–½ cup grated Parmesan cheese

lemon wedges to garnish

For the dressing, in a blender add the anchovies, garlic, egg yolks, red wine vinegar, Dijon Mustard, Worcestershire sauce, salt, and pepper. Blend on high, adding the olive oil in a slow steady stream to emulsify and make a thick, creamy dressing. Adding the oil too quickly will result in a runny, thin dressing. Refrigerate any leftover dressing in an airtight container for 3–5 days.

For the salad, in a large bowl, hand-tear the lettuce into desired sizes. I prefer larger pieces for presentation. Season to taste with the salt and pepper. Add Garlic Drizzle, Our Best Croutons, bacon, Parmesan cheese, and ¾ cup of dressing. Gently fold with a spatula until all the lettuce is evenly covered. Pile into tower-like presentations on individual plates and garnish each with a lemon wedge.

Make this a complete meal by adding a few pieces of smoked salmon, some capers, pulled pieces of barbecued chicken, or sliced steak. Be creative.

OUR BEST CROUTONS

Big, bold, and beautiful. That's the crouton for me. We use home-made focaccia—that's our house bread—which we cut into 1-inch cubes and bake until golden brown. Makes about 8 cups

1 loaf Our House Bread (page 78),
    crusty Italian bread, or your
    favourite bread, cut into
    1-inch cubes

1 cup olive oil
2 Tbsp garlic powder
kosher salt and freshly ground black
    pepper to taste

Preheat oven to 350°F.

In a large bowl, toss the bread cubes with the olive oil, garlic powder, and salt and pepper until evenly covered. Bake on a baking sheet for 15–18 minutes, or until all the croutons are evenly browned. Toss in with Marty's Killer Caesar Salad (page 57) or use as garnish on your favourite soup.

These can be stored in an airtight container for up to 30 days.

Café Confidential: Be sure to bake away all the moisture in the croutons—they should have a nice brownish colour. Moisture left in the croutons when stored has potential to develop mould and spoil.

MY FAVOURITE SIMPLE SALAD

This is my go-to salad that always tastes great, regardless of what I'm serving alongside. Serves 4

1 head red leaf lettuce, washed, dried,
    and hand-torn
2–3 green onions, chopped
1 tomato, cut into wedges
½ carrot, grated

large splash of balsamic vinegar
larger splash of extra virgin olive oil
kosher salt and freshly ground black
    pepper to taste

In a large bowl, add all the ingredients and toss gently. Pile high for appearance on individual plates. The sugars from the shredded carrot will add a subtle sweetness to this salad.

Café Confidential: Organic onions, tomatoes, and carrots really enhance the flavours of the salad. Garden fresh is ideal.

AYO'S MOUNTAIN SALAD

During my time in Spain with Ayo, he, seven of his staff, and I trekked for two hours into the mountains for the weekly run of mountain spring water. The spring rains in 1990 in the south of Spain had contaminated most of the local water supply and we had to fetch our own supplies for the restaurant. While we were filling the jugs with spring water, Ayo was busy creating this salad. Eating lunch while enjoying an incredible view of the Mediterranean Sea is something I'll always remember. Serves 4–6

4 ripe Haas avocados, pitted and sliced
2 tomatoes, cut into wedges
1 red onion, cubed
handful of black olives

juice of 1 lemon
½ cup olive oil
sea salt to taste

In a bowl, add all the ingredients and toss well to combine. We enjoyed this salad with fresh baguettes and red wine. Nice and simple.

MARTY'S WORLD FAMOUS BEAN SALAD

The **Toronto Star** tested and loved this recipe. You'll love it, too! Take this to your next picnic and wait for the compliments to come flooding in.

Serves 6–8

one 19 oz can chickpeas, drained

one 19 oz can red kidney beans, drained
  and rinsed

one 14 oz can cut green beans, drained

one 12 oz can whole kernel corn,
  undrained

¼ cup diced red onion

2½ Tbsp balsamic vinegar

6 cloves garlic, minced

3 Tbsp granulated sugar

2½ Tbsp dried basil

1½ tsp coarse kosher salt

1½ tsp freshly ground black pepper

6 Tbsp extra virgin olive oil

In a large bowl, combine the chickpeas, kidney beans, green beans, corn and its juices, and onion. In a small bowl, whisk together all the remaining ingredients, pour over the beans, and fold to combine. Refrigerate, covered, for at least 1 hour before serving.

Café Confidential: I often mix 4 cups of bean salad with 4 cups of rice or pasta for a variation. It's great as a side dish.

THE FAMILY POTATO SALAD

My oma, Elizabeth, unwittingly sparked a family competition to see who makes the best potato salad. This is a twist on my mother's version and it's simply fantastic. Friends often ask for the recipe and so here it is.
Serves 10–12

SALAD

5 lb whole potatoes, red or waxy variety

4 green onions, chopped

2 celery stalks, chopped fine

½ English cucumber, thinly sliced
   with skin on

7 radishes, thinly sliced

¾ cup chopped dill pickle

DRESSING

3 Tbsp red wine vinegar

1 egg yolk

1 garlic clove, crushed

2 tsp Dijon mustard

1½ tsp kosher salt

1 tsp freshly ground black pepper

½ cup olive oil

1 cup mayonnaise

¼ cup of pickle juice, or to taste

For the salad, add the potatoes to a large pot of salted boiling water and cook for 20–30 minutes, just until tender. Drain and let cool completely. Remove the skin, quarter the potatoes, and thinly slice each quarter. Transfer to a large bowl. Add the green onion, celery, cucumber, radishes, and dill pickle. Set aside.

For the dressing, in a bowl, whisk together the vinegar, egg yolk, garlic, mustard, salt, and pepper. Slowly add the olive oil, whisking constantly to emulsify the oil into the vinegar base, forming a thick mayonnaise-like texture.

Pour over the salad, and fold to coat evenly. Add the mayonnaise, and fold to coat evenly again. Add the desired amount of pickle juice for the texture you like and fold again. Season to taste with more salt and pepper.

I prefer a somewhat smooth, creamy texture rather than a sticky or runny texture. Let the salad rest for half an hour before serving. The flavours really come out on day 2. Refrigerate, covered, for up to 1 week.

Café Confidential: When making an emulsified sauce, you must add the oil in a slow, steady stream to avoid separation. Once an emulsion has formed and the sauce is beginning to thicken, then you can increase the speed with which you're adding the oil. This is an art and a science.

TED READER'S COLONEL MUSTARD'S SLAW

The great Canadian barbecue master, author, TV host, and all-round fun guy, Ted Reader, has generously allowed me to share with you his incredible coleslaw recipe. It comes from his book **On Fire in the Kitchen**. Thanks, Ted. Serves 6–8

½ head cabbage, thinly sliced
4 leaves mustard greens, thinly sliced
1 medium yellow bell pepper, thinly sliced
1 medium red onion, thinly sliced
3 green onions, thinly sliced
1 cup grated carrots
2 Tbsp chopped fresh parsley
½ cup vegetable oil

½ cup malt vinegar
2 Tbsp Dijon mustard
1 Tbsp dried mustard powder
1 Tbsp chopped fresh tarragon
1 Tbsp brown sugar
1 tsp yellow mustard seeds
1 tsp black mustard seeds
salt and freshly ground black pepper

In a large bowl, combine the cabbage, mustard greens, bell pepper, red onion, green onions, carrots, and parsley.

In a small saucepan, stir together the oil, vinegar, Dijon mustard, dried mustard powder, tarragon, sugar, and mustard seeds. Bring to a slow boil and simmer, stirring occasionally, for 5 minutes. Pour over the cabbage mixture. Toss to coat evenly. Season to taste with the salt and pepper.

Refrigerate, covered, for 2 hours before serving.

WARM GOAT CHEESE SALAD

This is another one of my favourite salads. It's rich in flavour, tastes fantastic with garlic bread or fresh baguettes, and can be served as a light meal. Serves 4

1 head green or red leaf lettuce,
  hand-torn
1 cup halved cherry tomatoes
1 cup English cucumber, thinly sliced
  with skin on
1 carrot, shredded
5 Tbsp olive oil
kosher salt and freshly ground
  black pepper to taste

2 cups sliced mushrooms
1 red onion, sliced
1 garlic clove, minced
⅓ cup balsamic vinegar
eight 2-inch round pieces
  fresh goat cheese
½ cup whole Candied Pecans
  (page 68)

In a salad bowl, combine the lettuce, cherry tomatoes, cucumber, carrot, 3 Tbsp of the olive oil, and salt and pepper. Toss gently.

Preheat broiler to high.

Heat the remaining olive oil in a saucepan over medium-high heat. Add the mushrooms, onion, and garlic, and sauté until the vegetables begin to caramelize, about 5 minutes. Add the balsamic vinegar. Stir and cook for 2–3 minutes.

Divide the lettuce mixture between 4 plates. Top with the onion and mushroom mixture with juices, 2 pieces of goat cheese, and pecans. Place under the broiler for 1 minute or just until the goat cheese softens. Serve.

CANDIED PECANS

These are great as a snack, on top of ice cream, or as garnish on salads—and they only take 10 minutes to make. Makes ½ cup

¼ cup brown sugar, packed

¼ cup water

½ cup whole pecans

In a small saucepan over high heat, add the sugar and water and bring to a boil. Using a whisk, start stirring constantly near the 8–9 minute mark as the sugar begins to bubble like hot candy. Working quickly, add the pecans, stir to cover them completely, and transfer to a greased cookie sheet, separating the nuts. Allow to cool completely.

Café Confidential: Use caution when working with boiled sugar. It's extremely hot.

CHICKPEA AND OLIVE SALAD

This protein-packed, good-carbohydrate mixture is great after a workout or as a backyard barbecue side dish. Try mixing it with pasta or rice.
Serves 4–6

two 19 oz cans chickpeas, drained
  and rinsed
¾ cup sliced green olives
¾ cup sliced black olives
½ red bell pepper, minced
½ cup olive or canola oil

juice of 1 lemon
3 Tbsp green olive juice
1 Tbsp fresh parsley
½ tsp granulated sugar
½ tsp kosher salt
¼ tsp freshly ground black pepper

In a bowl, add all the ingredients and fold to combine. Refrigerate in an airtight container for up to 5 days.

Café Confidential: Chickpeas, also known as garbanzo beans, are native to southwest Asia, but they're grown in Asia, Iran, Ethiopia, and Mexico. These versatile legumes are a staple foodstuff in vegetarian diets and are a main ingredient in several Middle Eastern and Indian dishes. They're also the oiliest of the legume family, coming in at 5% oil by weight, compared to most other legumes which are 1–2% oil by weight.

FRESH CUCUMBER AND DILL SALAD

It's difficult to beat the combined taste of fresh dill and chives from the garden, cucumber, and wine vinegar in this simple summery fresh salad. Serve this as a barbecue side dish, or enjoy it on its own as a light, low-fat snack. Serves 2–4

2 Tbsp wine vinegar, red or white

½ tsp Dijon mustard

3 Tbsp olive oil

1 Tbsp mayonnaise (optional)

1 English cucumber, thinly sliced with skin on

¼ cup chopped fresh dill

¼ cup chopped fresh chives

kosher salt and freshly ground black pepper to taste

In a bowl, whisk together the vinegar and Dijon mustard. Slowly whisk in the olive oil. Add the mayonnaise (if using) and whisk.

Add the cucumber, dill, and chives and fold to combine. Season to taste with salt and pepper.

MARTY'S GREEK SALAD

This is a very popular item at the café. Traditionally, it's served without lettuce. Try it both ways and see which you prefer. It's all about what you want! Makes 2–4 servings

½ English cucumber, cut with skin
　　on into ½-inch chunks
1 cup halved cherry tomatoes
1 cup crumbled feta cheese
½ cup kalamata olives
½ red bell pepper, cut into
　　½-inch chunks
½ small red onion, cut into
　　½-inch chunks

⅓ cup olive oil
1 small garlic clove, crushed
2 Tbsp dried oregano, rubbed
　　for fuller flavour
juice of ½ a lemon
kosher salt and freshly ground black
　　pepper to taste

In a bowl, toss all ingredients and combine well.

If you decide to serve it with lettuce, use romaine lettuce, and add Garlic Drizzle (page 56), more lemon juice, and salt and pepper to taste before tossing.

MARTY'S PERSONAL FAVOURITES

Some recipes are simply fun to make. They resonate with you, they become staples in your repertoire, and you usually enhance them to a higher level every time you make them. Here are a few that are fun for me, which I hope you try.

THE ORIGINAL BIG SANDWICH

One of the first food items that grabs your attention as you enter our store is the "Big Sandwich." Our bread is baked fresh daily, and the meat is piled high and adorned with just the right amount of toppings. Here's how you make it. Serves 8

1 loaf Our House Bread (page 78)
butter, enough to cover bottom half
   of bread
1 head iceberg lettuce, shredded or green
   leaf lettuce
2¼ lb black forest ham, shaved
2 whole tomatoes, sliced

½ red onion, thinly sliced
1 green bell pepper, thinly sliced
kosher salt and fresh ground black
   pepper to taste
mayonnaise to cover top half of bread
Dijon mustard (optional)

Cut our house bread in half lengthwise and open out. Cover the buttom half with the butter and add the lettuce. Add the ham in piles, the higher the better. Add the tomato, onion, green pepper, and salt and pepper. Cover the top half of the bread with mayo (adding some Dijon if you'd like), cover, and slice into 8 equal portions. Serve with soup or salad.

Café Confidential: This sandwich is also fantastic when baked in the oven at 350°F for 5–10 minutes or until the bread is toasted. Remove from the oven and lightly brush the top with Garlic Drizzle (page 56). The aroma alone is worth it.

OUR HOUSE BREAD

This is a very simple pizza-dough recipe that we shape focaccia style. Sometimes we alter the spices and toppings but we never change the formula. Makes 2 focaccia loaves

7 cups all-purpose flour
2 Tbsp granulated sugar
5 tsp dry active yeast
1½ Tbsp kosher salt
1 tsp freshly ground black pepper

2½ cups warm water
¼ cup olive oil
dried parsley (optional)
sea salt (optional)
chopped onion (optional)

In a stand mixer with a dough hook attachment, add the flour, sugar, yeast, salt, and pepper. Mix on speed 2 or low, and slowly add the warm water and ¼ cup olive oil. Mix for 8–10 minutes until the dough is creamy and smooth with some elasticity. Add a touch more water if it's too dry, or a little flour if it's too wet. You'll be able to tell which way to go around the 4–5 minute mark.

Preheat oven to 100°F.

Divide the dough into 2 evenly sized logs. Grease lightly with more olive oil and place on a large baking sheet. Cover with plastic wrap and let rise, until doubled in size, in the warm oven (or in the sun if you're lucky) for 25–30 minutes.

Unwrap and form into ¾-inch-high flat rectangular shapes, and sprinkle with dried parsley, sea salt, or chopped onion if using. Cover with the plastic wrap and let double in size again in the oven (or the sun). When doubled in size, remove the plastic wrap, increase oven to 350°F, and bake for 25–30 minutes. The edges will brown slightly and the middle will bounce back when pressed. Let cool in pan for half an hour.

Café Confidential: This recipe can also be mixed in a regular bowl and kneaded by hand on a floured surface for about 15 minutes.

Café Confidential: *Alternative Spices*
A tablespoon or two of any of these, when added to the flour, creates an entirely different flavour. Mix and match. Be creative.

- red chili flakes
- dried parsley
- onion flakes

- garlic powder
- oregano
- basil

- poppy seeds
- sunflower seeds
- flax seeds

Café Confidential: If you are using the dough as pizza dough, let it sit overnight in the fridge before stretching. The time will allow more flavour to develop. For a crunchier pizza crust, use bread flour instead of all-purpose. The higher the protein content, the more it will resemble real pizzeria crust. Hard flour is best and can be purchased from most food service suppliers.

THE ULTIMATE CANADIAN BACK BACON SANDWICH

Known for its unique flavour and peameal coating, Canadian back bacon is served at many farmers' markets and sandwich shops across Canada every day. Quick pan-frying seals in the juices and caramelizes the outer edges for the ultimate sandwich experience. Makes 4 sandwiches

1 Tbsp oil (more if needed when frying
    in batches)
12 thick slices peameal bacon

4 fresh Kaiser buns, halved
yellow or Dijon mustard
pickles on the side

Heat the oil in a skillet over medium-high heat. When the skillet is hot, add the bacon and cook 2 minutes per side or just until cooked throughout (not a minute longer). Layer slices on your bun, and serve with mustard, pickles, or your favourite condiment.

Café Confidential: *Condiment Ideas*
Try this sandwich with relish, ketchup, mayonnaise, sauerkraut, barbecue sauce, horseradish sauce, honey mustard, old Canadian cheddar, cranberry chutney, or diced onion.

THE $15 GRILLED CHEESE

This creation came by way of Randy Feltis, chef and owner of Oscar's Restaurant in Barrie, Ontario. We were comparing lunch menu items when he suggested I try his latest addition of exotic cheeses on thick-cut bread, slowly browned to perfection and served with a simple salad or soup. The $15 Grilled Cheese was born. Makes 4 sandwiches

½ cup butter, softened
3–4 garlic cloves, crushed
¼ cup chopped fresh parsley
8 slices fresh baked bread, ½ inch to
    1½ inches thick (Italian, potato,
    sourdough, cheese, whole-grain, or
    light rye bread)

8 slices brie cheese
8 slices aged cheddar cheese
8 slices Asiago cheese
8 slices havarti cheese

In a bowl, combine the butter, garlic, and parsley. Spread on 8 slices of the bread. In a large skillet over low heat, place 2 slices of bread, butter side down. Place 2 slices of each variety of cheese on top of the bread and cover with another piece of bread, butter side up. Cook the first side until golden brown, then flip and repeat. Covering the pan will help the cheese melt better, especially considering the thickness of the bread. When both sides are browned, cut on the diagonal and serve.

Café Confidential: Dill pickles, potato chips, and ketchup go well with this monster cheese fest. But if you're feeling creative, try adding prosciutto ham, salami, mortadella, black forest ham, shaved roast beef, or anything else that appeals to you. If you're using a thicker cut of bread, try covering the pan while cooking. It can help to melt the cheese properly. Send a photo of your greatest grilled cheese recipe to the contact address listed at www.martysworldfamous.com.

BIG ASS QUICHE

I once heard that real men don't eat quiche. Well, "real men" eat what they want to eat and this real man wants quiche. In fact, it's one of our best-selling lunch items. This recipe has a light and fluffy texture in a unique phyllo pastry. It's also super-easy to make. Makes 1 Big Ass Quiche or two 10-inch quiches • Serves 8–12

½ cup butter, melted
1 large leek, washed and chopped
1½ cups chopped, thinly sliced ham
16 eggs
2 cups 10% cream
1½ Tbsp parsley, dried
1 tsp fresh ground pepper

½ tsp kosher salt
½ tsp nutmeg
8 large sheets of phyllo pastry
2 cups shredded mozzarella
½ cup grated fresh Parmesan
salt and freshly ground pepper to sprinkle
　　on the rim

Preheat oven to 350°F.

In a large skillet on medium-high heat, add ¼ cup of the butter. Then add the leek and sauté for 5 minutes. Add the ham and sauté for 5–10 minutes until the leeks and ham caramelize and brown slightly. Remove from heat. Set aside.

In a large bowl, whisk the eggs, then add the cream and whisk to combine. Add the parsley, pepper, salt, and nutmeg. Whisk to combine.

Brush the bottom and sides of a Marty's pan, or two deep-dish 10-inch pie plates, with some of the remaining butter. Add 1 layer of phyllo pastry at time, brushing each layer with some reserved butter. Criss-cross each sheet of phyllo and press them into the bottom of the pan, lifting the corners.

Place the leek and ham, then the cheeses, on top of the phyllo. Add the egg mixture, and lightly season the phyllo edges with salt and pepper. Bake for 40 minutes or until the centre is firm. If you're making 2 smaller quiches, check them after 30 minutes.

Serve with a My Favourite Simple Salad (page 59) or Opa's Mushroom Soup (page 52).

Café Confidential: Substitute old Canadian cheddar or Gruyère cheese for the mozzarella.

EASY VEGGIE PIZZA

We've sold literally thousands of these tasty pizzas over the years. They work well as an appetizer but with a fresh Caesar or Greek salad on the side, they make a great light vegetarian meal. Makes 6 pizzas

6 Greek-style pitas
6 Tbsp Garlic Drizzle (page 56)
3 cups shredded mozzarella cheese, plus
    12 Tbsp for sprinkling
6 tsp dried oregano
1 red onion, sliced thinly

1 green bell pepper, cut into
    chunky slices
2 tomatoes, cut into chunky slices
sea salt and freshly cracked black
    pepper to taste

Preheat oven to 400°F.

Lay out the pitas on a cookie sheet and drizzle each pita with 1 Tbsp Garlic Drizzle. Add ½ cup of the mozzarella cheese, 1 tsp of the oregano, and slices of the onion, green pepper, and tomato to each pita. Season to taste with the salt and pepper.

Sprinkle 2 tablespoons of mozzarella on top of each pita.

Bake for 8–10 minutes, or until golden brown.

Café Confidential: Create your own pizza by trying these toppings: portobello mushrooms, green or black olives, feta cheese, basil, broccoli, zucchini, anchovies, artichoke hearts, bell peppers (red, yellow, or orange). The possibilities are endless. You can also try spreading a light layer of Mario Batali's Basic Tomato Sauce (page 91) on the pita before adding the toppings.

MARINATED CHICKEN WRAPS

This is another Marty's staple that people can't get enough of. Full of flavour, these soft, warm wraps are perfect for quick school lunches or even picnics. Serves 6

1 whole barbecue chicken (most
    supermarkets prepare them now)
5 Tbsp soy sauce
2 Tbsp garlic powder
6 Greek-style pitas
6 romaine lettuce leaves
6 Tbsp mayonnaise

¼ cup thinly sliced red onion
1 tomato, cut in half and sliced thinly
¼ cup thinly sliced green bell pepper
kosher salt and freshly ground black
    pepper to taste
Garlic Drizzle (page 56)

Remove the meat from the chicken. In a large bowl, tear the meat into smaller strand-like pieces. Add the soy sauce and garlic powder and fold to combine.

This next step needs to be completed quickly, otherwise the pitas can become hard and brittle. Warm the pitas in their bag for 1½–2 minutes, or until soft and pliable. Place all 6 pitas on a counter and top each with 1 leaf of the lettuce. Place 1 Tbsp of the mayonnaise on the centre of each lettuce leaf. Add a handful of chicken, and slices of the onion, tomato, and green pepper. Season to taste with the salt and pepper.

Still working quickly, take a 12- × 12-inch piece of waxed paper. From the top edge down, folding twice, form a 1-inch strengthened top band. This will help secure each wrap. Slide this reinforced band under the wrap to halfway. Fold the wrap in half, tighten the waxed paper, and twist the bottom securely. This will keep the wrap intact with no risk of it falling apart. Warm the wraps in the microwave oven for 30 seconds, then pour a little Garlic Drizzle overtop just before serving. Try them with your favourite hot sauce, as well.

TOASTED SMOKED SALMON PITA WITH CAPERS AND RED ONION

This is an undisputed favourite among Marty's patrons. We are visited every year by two men who come in just for this very sandwich and a bowl of Marty's Red Pepper Soup (page 49) as part of their annual fishing trip weekend. "When the fish aren't biting . . . we can always get some at Marty's." Make this once and you'll probably make it again.

Makes 4 sandwiches

4 Greek-style pitas
12 Tbsp cream cheese
8–12 large slices smoked salmon
4 tsp capers
red onion, thinly sliced

sea salt and freshly ground black pepper, to taste
Garlic Drizzle (page 56)
grated lemon rind (optional)
fresh squeezed lemon juice (optional)
fresh dill (optional)

Cut each pita in half. On one half only, spread 3 Tbsp of the cream cheese. Add 2–3 slices of the smoked salmon, 1 tsp of the capers, some thin slices of the red onion, and salt and pepper to taste. Cover with the other pita half, and toast or broil in a toaster oven until you have your desired doneness. Brush with Garlic Drizzle. If you like, add some grated lemon rind, lemon juice, and fresh dill for extra zing. Savour with soup or salad.

Café Confidential: *Cut Onions, Cry Less*
Someone once told me that if I wet my hands before cutting an onion, my eyes wouldn't water. It turns out that onion vapour is attracted to moisture like that of your eye. Whenever your cutting board and hands are wet, the vapour is attracted to them instead. It works. Also, lean away from your cutting board, so if the vapour is rising, it will rise in front of you instead of directly at you.

MARIO BATALI'S BASIC TOMATO SAUCE

For years I've enjoyed the way Mario Batali has prepared Italian pasta, and I particularly love the simplicity of many of his recipes. He's allowed me to share with you one of my personal favourites, his basic tomato sauce from his fabulous book **Molto Italiano**. After watching Mario prepare linguini, I now always finish my pasta with fresh chopped flat-leafed parsley, Parmesan (preferably Parmigiano Reggiano), and a splash of good olive oil. Thank you, Mario. Make 4 cups

¼ cup extra virgin olive oil

1 Spanish onion, cut into ¼-inch dice

4 garlic cloves, thinly sliced

3 Tbsp chopped fresh thyme

½ medium carrot, shredded fine

two 28 oz cans whole tomatoes

salt to taste

In a 3-quart saucepan, heat the olive oil over medium heat. Add the onion and garlic and cook until soft and light golden brown, about 8–10 minutes. Add the thyme and carrot and cook until the carrot is quite soft, about 5 minutes.

Add the tomatoes with their juice and bring to a boil, stirring often. Lower the heat and simmer until the sauce is as thick as hot cereal, about half an hour. Season to taste with salt. The sauce can be refrigerated for up to 1 week or frozen for 6 months.

Café Confidential: *My Favourite Pasta*
Rustichella d'abruzzo is the best-tasting brand of dried pasta I've eaten. It's imported by Brunello Imports Inc. (416-631-9773 or email them at brunello@colosseum.com), and it's gradually becoming more readily available in finer boutique grocery stores. Made from 100% durham wheat semolina, this pasta is so flavourful it could almost be eaten without a sauce. I hope you have a chance to try it. Remember to cook it for 1 minute less than the recommended cooking time for *al dente*.

GUACAMOLE

This is my all-time favourite appetizer. I learned it from a Mexican restaurateur and it's one of the earliest recipes I memorized. It's always a huge hit at parties and gatherings. Toasted tortilla chips are the perfect finishing touch. Enjoy. Serves 4

2 ripe Haas avocados, peeled and pitted
1 ripe organic tomato, diced
1 small red onion, minced
1 clove garlic, minced
½ bunch cilantro, washed and chopped
juice of ½ a lime

½–1 jalapeño pepper, seeded and
    finely minced
2 Tbsp olive oil
kosher salt and fresh ground black
    pepper to taste
1 large bag restaurant-style tortilla
    chips to serve

In a bowl, add all the avocados, tomato, onion, garlic, cilantro, lime juice, jalapeño, olive oil, and salt and pepper to taste. Mash with a fork or potato masher. Let stand for 1 hour for the flavours to fully develop.

Toast the tortilla chips on a cookie sheet under the broiler just until the edges brown slightly. Set out a round platter with tortilla chips and place a bowl of the guacamole in the middle of the platter. *¡Ay caramba!*

BIG ASS SALSA

Organic tomatoes and an explosion of fresh herbs, peppers, and citrus will have you casting your manners out the window and dipping with both hands. Perfect for a great party or summer get-together. Makes 3 cups

5–6 organic tomatoes
1¼ cups finely chopped red onion
¾ cup chopped cilantro
½ red bell pepper, minced
½ green bell pepper, minced
½ yellow bell pepper, minced
½ orange bell pepper, minced
2 jalapeño peppers, seeded and
   chopped fine
4 green onions, chopped, both white
   and green parts

4 garlic cloves, crushed
juice of 1 lemon
juice of 2 limes
1½ Tbsp kosher salt
1 Tbsp Tabasco sauce
1 tsp cumin
½ tsp white pepper
½ tsp brown sugar, packed
one 14 oz can tomato sauce to
   thicken (optional)

In a large bowl, add all of the ingredients except the tomato sauce and fold to combine. Gradually add some of the tomato sauce if you like a lighter texture, but try it without first. Serve with toasted corn chips or toasted pita wedges.

POUTINE

This recipe is as Canadian as it gets, and so is the story of its origins. In the fall of 1957, Quebec restaurateur Fernand Lachance, owner of Le Lutin Qui Rit ("the laughing goblin") in Warwick, Quebec, took a special request from a regular customer, Eddy Lanesse, for a plate of fries topped with cheese and brown gravy. Lachance prepared the dish as requested and called his creation **poutine**, local slang for "a real mess." It tastes fantastic. Just don't tell your doctor. Serves 4

3 or 4 baking potatoes
2 cups peanut oil
1 package gravy mix, dark beef variety

2 cups white cheese curds
kosher salt and freshly ground black
    pepper to taste

Wash the potatoes and cut them into ¼-inch strips, and submerge in water for at least half an hour. Longer is better.

In a large, high-walled saucepan over medium-high heat, add the peanut oil and heat the oil to a consistent 300°F. Use a thermometer if you have one.

Pat the potatoes dry with a paper towel and fry in small batches just until limp, about 5 minutes. Remove with a slotted spoon and drain on a paper towel.

Preheat oven to 300°F. Line a cookie sheet with paper towel.

Increase the oil temperature to 375°F or high heat for final frying. Finish frying all the potatoes until golden brown and keep them warm on the prepared cookie sheet in the oven until needed.

Prepare the gravy as per the package instructions. Set aside and keep warm. Reheat before serving.

Arrange the fries on a platter or plate, top with the cheese curds, and cover with the hot gravy. Season to taste. Malt vinegar and ketchup could be in order here. A real fine mess indeed! Wait until you taste it.

SIMPLE WINGS

Legend has it that one evening the owners of the Anchor Bar in Buffalo, New York, were about to close when their son and some friends arrived hungry after a night on the town. The kitchen had pretty much been cleaned up for the evening. The only thing left on was the deep fryer and a pile of chicken wings about to be boiled for soup stock. The mother deep-fried the wings and rolled them in hot sauce, butter, and vinegar. Buffalo Wings were born and the Anchor Bar remains their official birthplace. What was once often thrown away is now the most popular part of the bird. Using fresh chicken wings makes a big difference in the flavour and texture.
Serves 4 couch potatoes

2 cups all-purpose flour

1 Tbsp kosher salt

1 Tbsp freshly ground black pepper

1 Tbsp garlic powder

4 lb fresh chicken wings, tips removed

2 cups peanut oil

In a plastic bag combine the flour, salt, pepper, and garlic powder and shake well. Add the wings and shake until they're completely covered.

Preheat oven to 300°F.

In a large, deep saucepan, heat the peanut oil to 375°F or medium-high heat. Add the coated wings in batches, turning once after 8 or 9 minutes, and cook for a total of 16–18 minutes or until golden and crispy. Remove from the oil with a slotted spoon and drain off any excess oil in a paper towel–lined bowl or plate. Keep warm in the oven until all the wings are cooked.

AWESOME WING SAUCE
Makes about 1 cup

4–6 Tbsp your favourite hot sauce
4 Tbsp butter
4 Tbsp white or cider vinegar

In a small saucepan over medium-high heat, melt the sauce ingredients and stir to combine. Put the chicken wings in a bowl, pour sauce overtop, and toss to cover. Serve platter-style with celery sticks and blue cheese dressing on the side.

This is my favourite Super Bowl appetizer to put me in the mood for the big game.

INCREDIBLE IRISH PUB STEW

With an Irish last name like Curtis, it's only fitting that I should pay tribute to my ancestry with this incredibly flavourful recipe. Guinness and good red wine complete its richness and depth. I urge you to try it. Why wait until March 17? Serves 4–6

¼ cup olive oil

1¼ lb tri-tip beef, cut into 1-inch cubes

7 cloves garlic, minced

6 cups beef stock

1 cup red wine

1 cup Guinness

3 Tbsp chopped fresh thyme

2 Tbsp tomato paste

1 Tbsp Worcestershire sauce

1 Tbsp maple syrup or brown sugar

1–2 bay leaves

3 Tbsp butter

4 large baking potatoes, peeled
   and cut into ½-inch cubes

3 large carrots, peeled and cut into
   ½-inch pieces

1 large onion, chopped

kosher salt and freshly ground pepper
   to taste

chopped fresh parsley for garnish

In a large pot over medium-high heat, add the oil and brown the meat on all sides, about 5–7 minutes. Add the garlic and stir for 1 minute. Add the beef stock, wine, beer, thyme, tomato paste, Worcestershire sauce, maple syrup, and bay leaves. Stir and bring to a boil. Reduce the heat to low and simmer for 1 hour, partially covered, and stir occasionally.

Meanwhile, in a large saucepan over medium heat, melt the butter and add the potatoes, carrots, and onion. Stir until golden, about 20 minutes. Set aside.

After the beef has simmered for 1 hour, add the vegetables to the stew, stir, and simmer, uncovered, for 40 minutes.

Remove the bay leaves, and spoon off any excess fat. Season to taste with salt and pepper, and sprinkle the parsley to garnish. Get out the bread for dipping.

Café Confidential: Guinness was first brewed back in 1759 in a Dublin brewery owned by Arthur Guinness. The brewery is on record as being the first to be incorporated as a public company on the London Stock Exchange in 1886.

TEXAS-STYLE CHAMPIONSHIP CHILI

Authentic Texas chili is serious business for chiliheads who compete throughout North America annually for the $25,000 first prize. This recipe gives accurate techniques and ingredients that will make you the chili champion amongst friends and family. A good butcher will provide you with the all-important tri-tip beef. Remember that true Texas chili is made without beans. Serves 12–16 chili fanatics

SPICE

4 Tbsp mild chili powder

4 Tbsp medium ancho chili powder

3 Tbsp cumin

2 Tbsp chipotle chili powder

2 tsp kosher salt

1 tsp freshly ground black pepper

1 tsp oregano

MEAT

3 lb tri-tip beef, cubed

1 tsp kosher salt

½ tsp freshly ground black pepper

3 Tbsp peanut oil

1 lb pork shoulder, cubed

HEAT

1 Tbsp peanut oil

1 white onion, minced

7 garlic cloves, minced

1 jalapeño pepper, seeded and minced
  fine

1 medium hot yellow pepper, seeded and
  minced fine

4 cups chicken stock

one 7 oz can green jalapeño chilies

1 cup tomato sauce

SWEET

1 Tbsp brown sugar, rounded

juice of 1 lime

For the spice, mix together all the ingredients and set aside.

For the meat, season the cubed beef with the salt and pepper. In a large stockpot over medium heat, add the peanut oil, then brown the beef in small batches, and reserve. Brown the pork in the same oil and reserve.

To the same pot, add the 1 Tbsp peanut oil, onion, garlic, jalapeño pepper, and yellow pepper and sweat for 5 minutes. Add the reserved beef and pork, 2 cups of the chicken stock, the can of chilies, ½ cup of the tomato sauce, and half of the reserved spices. Be sure to stir, lifting any caramelized beef bits from the bottom of the pot. Bring to a boil, cover, and reduce the heat to a simmer for 1½ hours.

Add the remaining spices, 2 cups of chicken stock, and ½ cup of tomato sauce and simmer, slightly covered, for another hour, stirring occasionally.

Lastly, add the brown sugar and lime juice and simmer, slightly uncovered, for half an hour. This will round out all the flavours and balance the chili.

Serve with Roasted Garlic Bread (page 98). Enjoy.

ROASTED GARLIC BREAD

This garlic bread has a smooth, garlicky, nutty flavour and goes great with . . . well, just about anything. Perfect for Marty's Killer Caesar Salad (page 57) or Warm Goat Cheese Salad (page 66). Serves 4

1 head garlic (7–10 cloves)
3 Tbsp butter, softened

1 large baguette, halved or sliced
   diagonally

Preheat oven to 350°F.

Bake 1 head of garlic in its skin on a baking sheet until browned, about half an hour. Preheat broiler to high.

Cool the garlic for 5 minutes (it should still be warm), peel, and then chop and add to the butter. Stir together and evenly spread over the baguette. Place under broiler until golden.

Experiment with mozzarella cheese on top, some oregano, basil, or parsley in the butter, or anything else that tickles your fancy.

GNOCCHI WITH PROSCIUTTO AND CREMINI MUSHROOMS

I once had this dish in Huntsville, Ontario. I sat with a glass of red wine in my hand and watched the sunset over the Muskoka River. This was one of the most enjoyable meals I have eaten in Muskoka. It's also surprisingly quick and easy to make. If you have all the fresh ingredients at hand you'll be able to produce this in 20 minutes. Serves 4

6 cups lightly salted water

3 Tbsp olive oil

½ white onion, diced

4 cloves garlic, thinly sliced

1 cup chopped cremini mushrooms

2 Roma tomatoes, diced

½ tsp kosher salt

¼ tsp freshly ground black pepper

2 Tbsp red wine

4 Tbsp chopped fresh basil

1 Tbsp butter

1 lb gnocchi

4–6 slices prosciutto, chopped

2 Tbsp fresh parsley

Bring the salted water to a boil. Meanwhile, heat a large saucepan over medium heat, add the oil, onion, garlic, and mushrooms. Sauté for 3–5 minutes until slightly browned. Add the tomatoes, salt, and pepper, and stir for 2–3 minutes. Add the wine and cook for 1–2 minutes to boil off the alcohol. Add the basil and butter and stir. Reduce the heat to low.

Gently drop the gnocchi into the boiling water. Gnocchi is cooked when it starts to float, 3–5 minutes. Remove the cooked gnocchi from the water with a slotted spoon and add to the sauce in the saucepan. Stir to coat, adding a little gnocchi water if you prefer a thinner sauce. Toss in the prosciutto and parsley, fold gently to mix, and serve immediately.

Top with freshly grated Parmesan and a splash of Garlic Drizzle (page 56) or olive oil. This is fantastic with Roasted Garlic Bread (page 98) and My Favourite Simple Salad (page 59).

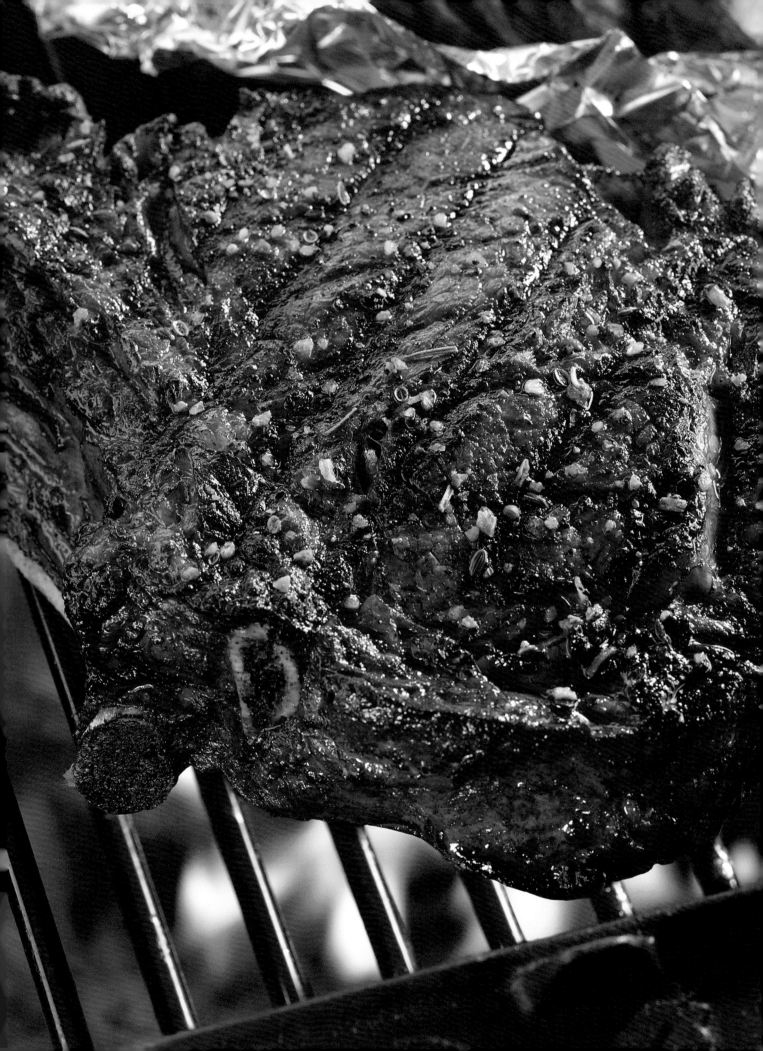

BARBECUE CLASSICS

For almost all Canadians, barbecue and summer go hand in hand. There's no doubt that in Muskoka, the barbecue is king in the summer. Long sunny days playing in and around the lake can sure create an appetite, and here are a few recipes that I enjoy with friends and family all summer long. So fire up the barbecue and experience the love. Try them all.

A TRIVIAL MARINADE

I learned this marinade from Chris Haney, co-inventor of Trivial Pursuit, one evening as he prepared dinner for a gathering in Caledon, Ontario. It works on beef, chicken, and pork. It's my favourite. It's also nice and simple. Makes 1 cup

½ cup soy sauce

½ cup olive oil

1 Tbsp black pepper

1 Tbsp garlic, powder or fresh crushed

In a bowl, combine all the ingredients and whisk well. Pour overtop steaks, chicken, or pork in a glass container, cover, and refrigerate for 1–48 hours, depending on the strength of flavour you desire. I prefer overnight.

MY BBQ SAUCE

There was a time, not so long ago, when I was consumed with wanting to learn and master everything there was to know about barbecue. It all started when I bought a new smoker. Three authors helped make experimenting with my new toy more fun: Ronnie Shewchuk, author of **Barbecue Secrets**, Ted Reader, author of **On Fire in the Kitchen**, and Steven Raichlen, author of the **Barbecue! Bible** series. These guys really know their stuff and with their help, creating my own barbecue sauce was fun and rewarding. Makes 2 cups

⅓ cup olive oil
7 garlic cloves, minced
½ cup finely chopped onion
1 organic tomato, diced fine
¼ cup cider vinegar
¾ cup ketchup
½ cup Coke
⅓ cup yellow mustard
2 Tbsp Buttertart BBQ Rub (page 107)
1 Tbsp brown sugar

2 tsp cumin
1 tsp dried mustard powder
1 tsp kosher salt
1 tsp Worcestershire sauce
½ tsp cinnamon
½ tsp ancho chili powder
½ tsp freshly ground black pepper
¼ tsp cayenne
few dashes Tabasco

Heat the olive oil in a saucepan over medium heat. Add the garlic and onion, and sauté for about 5 minutes until softened. Add the tomato and cook until soft, about 5 minutes. Add the vinegar and stir for 1 minute. Add the remaining ingredients and bring to a boil. Reduce the heat and simmer for 5–10 minutes to thicken. Stir.

I especially love this sauce on ribs and chicken. Finish with barbecue sauce near the last half hour of your cooking time. Re-glaze just before serving. Refrigerate any leftover sauce for up to 1 month.

Café Confidential: I've discovered that using indirect low heat for chicken and ribs in your gas grill not only keeps the juices in, but it also reduces the risk of overcooking and burning the meat.

MONTREAL STEAK SPICE

This famous seasoning is loaded with unique flavours that can turn an ordinary steak into an incredible steak. Try it on potatoes or pork as well.
Makes ¾ cup

2 Tbsp kosher salt

2 Tbsp freshly cracked black pepper

2 Tbsp paprika

1 Tbsp crushed red pepper flakes

1 Tbsp crushed coriander

1 Tbsp dill

1 Tbsp garlic powder

1 Tbsp onion powder

In a bowl, combine all the ingredients and mix well. Store leftover spice in an airtight jar for up to 6 months. To use it, simply sprinkle the desired amount directly onto your steaks before grilling.

Café Confidential: For something different mix 3 Tbsp steak spice with ½ cup soy sauce and ½ cup olive oil. Marinate steaks overnight.

BUTTERTART BBQ RUB

One day I was inspired to create a great-tasting barbecue rub using the sweetness of our buttertarts. All modesty aside, I think this could be my greatest creation yet. It works for chicken, ribs, and pork and is my go-to seasoning all summer long. Makes 1 cup

½ cup kosher salt

¼ cup brown sugar

2 tsp garlic powder

1 tsp onion powder

1 tsp chili powder

1 tsp sweet paprika

1 tsp ground cumin

1 tsp dried mustard powder

1 tsp cinnamon

¾ tsp black pepper

Combine all the ingredients.

   Before applying the rub, coat your meat with Dijon or yellow mustard, just like the pros. Then sprinkle rub all over and barbecue as desired.

Café Confidential: Keep this rub in an airtight glass jar for a maximum of 6 months. And remember to label the jar!

BUTTERTART BBQ SAUCE

If you love both buttertarts and barbecue, then you'll also love this
Buttertart BBQ Sauce. I introduced this sauce to friends and family at a
barbecue get-together on Lake Simcoe. One friend described it as having
"encore flavour," a flavour that you keep wanting more of. Thanks, Captain
Bob, for those honest and kind words. See you on the lake. Makes 1 cup

1 head garlic
½ cup brown sugar, packed
¼ cup butter
¼ cup water

1 Tbsp Buttertart BBQ Rub (page 107)
juice of ¼ lemon
⅛ tsp nutmeg

Preheat oven to 350°F.

Bake the whole head of garlic (in its skin) on a cookie sheet for half an hour. Cool,
then peel and chop about 10 cloves, more if you like.

In a saucepan on medium to high heat, melt the sugar and butter. Add the remaining
ingredients, stir, and bring to a boil for 5 minutes. Reduce the heat, simmer for 5
minutes, and stir occasionally. Let cool.

Use this to glaze chicken, ribs, or pork in the final stages of cooking.

STEVEN RAICHLEN'S CHINESE BBQ SAUCE

This unique sauce adds a whole new twist to ribs and chicken, and comes from the pages of Steven Raichlen's **Barbecue! Bible: Sauces, Rubs, and Marinades, Bastes, Butters, and Glazes.** Check out his website at www.barbecuebible.com. I always feel inspired by his books. I know you will too. Makes 1 cup

½ cup hoisin sauce

3 Tbsp Chinese rice wine, sake, or dry sherry

2 Tbsp soy sauce

2 Tbsp granulated or brown sugar

2 Tbsp ketchup

2 Tbsp minced garlic

1 Tbsp rice wine vinegar or white vinegar

Bring all the ingredients to a boil in a small saucepan. Reduce the heat and simmer for 5 minutes. Use this sauce to brush chicken and ribs during the last half hour of their cooking time and re-glaze before serving.

BUTTERTART BURGERS

Sweet, savoury, juicy, and incredible. This is an entirely new barbecue sensation that will definitely have people talking. The combination of lean ground beef and pork gives this burger a softer texture. Definitely worth trying. Makes 6–8 burgers

1 lb ground sirloin or lean ground beef

1 lb ground pork

½ cup diced onion

⅓ cup brown sugar, packed

¼ cup dry bread crumbs

2 egg whites

2 cloves garlic, crushed

3 Tbsp Buttertart BBQ Rub (page 107)

2 Tbsp butter, melted

1 Tbsp freshly squeezed lemon juice

2 tsp dried mustard powder

1 tsp vanilla

½ tsp nutmeg

In a large bowl combine all the ingredients and mix well with your hands. Form the patties into the desired size and barbecue, or cook in 3 Tbsp oil in a stovetop skillet on medium heat until browned on both sides.

Café Confidential: This burger is fantastic with The Family Potato Salad (page 64), Ted Reader's Colonel Mustard's Slaw (page 65), or My Favourite Simple Salad (page 59).

RIBS 101

After years of experimenting with rib techniques, I've found that this method works extremely well for me. This is based on methods used by the professionals in competition except that in this recipe we use the grill instead of a smoker. I love to eat this with Is That Potato in My Mashed Garlic? (page 123) and My Favourite Simple Salad (page 59). This is real food for the soul, and it's also a Muskoka summer tradition for me, my friends, and my family. Serves 4–8

4 racks meaty pork back ribs
yellow mustard

⅓ cup Buttertart BBQ Rub (page 107)
2 cups Buttertart BBQ Sauce (page 108)

PREPARE THE GRILL
Low and slow is the rule here. A low temperature of 200–225°F is ideal for cooking great ribs. This temperature will allow the fibres in the meat to relax as it cooks, thus holding in all the essential juices. One burner on low should create this temperature. A thermometer is a must. Remember, great ribs take time, and patience will produce the best results.

PREPARE THE RIBS
Remove any excess fat. Peel off the membrane from the pork back side of the ribs by lifting one corner, then grabbing it with a paper towel. Pull slowly. This allows the flavours from the mustard and rub seasoning to be absorbed into both sides of the ribs.

Rub the ribs on both sides with a light coating of yellow mustard. This creates a more intense flavour and acts as a base for the rub to adhere to.

Sprinkle the ribs on both sides with the Buttertart BBQ Rub.

COOK THE RIBS
Place the ribs meaty side up on the upper rack of the grill (or alternatively, on the cold side of the grill). Keep the lid closed.

After about 2 hours, rotate the ribs to avoid burning the bottoms. After 3 hours total cooking time, cover both sides of the ribs with the Buttertart BBQ Sauce, wrap loosely in aluminum foil, and seal tightly. Cook for 1 more hour.

Remove the ribs from the grill and let stand for 10–15 minutes with the foil top slightly open. This allows the fibres in the meat to relax and absorb all the natural juices.

Remove the foil. Cut and serve with any remaining Buttertart BBQ Sauce.

TENDER BEEF BRISKET

This recipe is famous in Texas for a reason. Slow cooking over indirect heat (200–225°F) produces a tender, melt-in-your-mouth, juicy meat, perfect for barbecue gatherings. Try this recipe and experience the love. Makes 8 to 10 lb • Serves 8–12

½ cup sweet paprika
½ cup brown sugar, packed
½ cup kosher salt
3 Tbsp garlic powder
3 Tbsp onion powder

2 Tbsp oregano
1 tsp cayenne pepper
8–10 lb beef brisket, fat cap on
   (ask your butcher)
yellow mustard

In a bowl, combine all the spices and mix well.

Rub both sides of the brisket with yellow mustard. Sprinkle over the desired amount of spices and rub into the meat for full flavour. Preheat gas grill or smoker to 200–225°F. One burner on your grill at the very lowest setting should produce this temperature range. It's important to maintain this temperature throughout for maximum tenderness.

Place the brisket, fat side up, on the warming rack above the grill. Close the lid. Cook for 5–6 hours, or until the thickest part of brisket reads 170°F on a meat thermometer. Rotate the brisket, if necessary, to prevent one side from becoming overcooked underneath. Do not flip it. The fat cap slowly bastes the brisket during the cooking process. Barbecue Law #1: If you're lookin', you ain't cookin'. Keep the lid closed as much as possible.

Allow the brisket to rest, tented in aluminum foil, for 20 minutes to allow the juices to settle. Cut across the grain for maximum tenderness.

Serve thinly sliced on top of a salad, pile it high on a bun, or wrap it.

Café Confidential: Low-temperature cooking allows the fibres in the meat to relax. This is crucial for optimum tenderness and juiciness. We've all seen meat when scorched by high heat—it tightens and dries out. Not pretty. Also keep a spray bottle of apple juice, or a mixture of apple juice and whisky, handy to moisten the meat every hour, if desired.

Store any leftover spices in an airtight jar or freezer bag. Remember to label it.

MEN'S NIGHT STEAK SANDWICH

Wednesday night Men's Night at South Muskoka Golf and Curling Club is always filled with fun, good company, and good food. Inspired by the Food Network's piece on the "Filly" Steak Sandwich, I reintroduced the guys to a twist on our weekly steak dinner. Makes 1 hungry-man sandwich

1 New York strip loin
Montreal Steak Spice (page 106) or
　Buttertart BBQ Rub (page 107) to
　season

8-inch fresh baguette, cut in half
　lengthwise
Garlic Drizzle (page 56)
My Barbecue Sauce (page 105) or
　your favourite barbecue sauce

Preheat gas grill to medium-high.

　With a sharp fillet knife, cut the steak lengthwise into 2 thin halves. Place on a cutting board and tenderize with a meat hammer. Season both pieces with Montreal Steak Spice or Buttertart BBQ Rub and grill for 3 minutes per side on the gas grill. Brush the baguette with Garlic Drizzle and toast on the grill. Stack both pieces of steak between the baguette halves and brush on the barbecue sauce.

Café Confidential: Sautéed onions added to this sandwich are amazing: in a skillet over medium heat, sauté 1 sliced onion with 1 Tbsp of Buttertart BBQ Rub (page 107) in 3 Tbsp butter until the onions are golden brown. Serving the sandwich with the onions and melted Swiss cheese will bring it over the top. Enjoy.

KILLER RIB STEAK

What would summer in Muskoka be like without a perfectly cooked, thick, tender, and juicy rib steak? Boring, that's what! A properly cooked rib steak is a true sign of a barbecue aficionado.

So, spoil yourself. Ask your butcher for a 1½- to 2-inch-thick rib steak, bone in, and get out your camera. It's picture perfect when finished. Allow yourself 24–48 hours to marinate the steaks. Serves 2 to 4

two 1½–2 inch rib steaks, bone in   2 cups Trivial Marinade (page 104)

In a glass casserole dish, add the steaks and cover with the marinade. Flip a few times to thoroughly cover the steaks. Cover with plastic wrap and refrigerate for 6–48 hours.

Think about what you'd like to serve with the steaks. Pick out a great red wine and make sure you're not rushed.

Heat the grill for 20 minutes on high heat, then brush it clean and grease lightly with oil and paper towel where the steaks will go. Turn off the heat on one side. Sear the steaks for 1–2 minutes per side on the hot side of the grill. Then transfer to the cool side, close the lid, and essentially bake the steaks until you achieve the desired doneness.

Have a spray bottle of water handy for flare-ups.

Remove the steaks from the grill and let rest for 10 minutes to allow the juices to settle and return into the meat fibres.

I'd love to see your pictures of this feast. Please send them along to the contact address listed at www.martysworldfamous.com.

Café Confidential: I've found that quickly searing meat seals in its juices. You can then transfer it to a cooler area of the grill to perfectly "bake" the steak until finished. Many famous steak houses and chefs believe that a rib steak should be served rare to medium-rare at most . . . and most times *bleu* if you can handle it.

BUTTERTART CHICKEN

This recipe was the talk of the town when I made it for staff and neighbours at the café one afternoon. It's so simple and scrumptious. It goes great with My Favourite Simple Salad (page 59) or The Family Potato Salad (page 64). Serves 4–6

6 chicken quarters (leg and thigh)

6 Tbsp Dijon mustard

6 tsp Buttertart BBQ Rub (page 107)

1 cup Buttertart BBQ Sauce (page 108)

Preheat your gas grill to 300°F by heating one burner on or near the lowest setting.

Cover each piece of the chicken with 1 Tbsp Dijon mustard and 1 tsp Buttertart BBQ Rub.

Place on the upper rack of your grill, skin side up, and cook for 45–60 minutes. Glaze with the Buttertart BBQ Sauce and cook for an additional 15–20 minutes or until centre is no longer pink. Re-glaze and remove from the grill. Let stand for at least 5 minutes before serving.

Café Confidential: This recipe can also be prepared in the oven. Roast the chicken in a 350°F oven for 1 hour on a baking sheet. Remove and glaze the chicken with Buttertart BBQ Sauce, and finish roasting for 15–20 minutes. Remove and let stand for 5 minutes before serving. Serve with extra barbecue sauce for dipping.

CANDIED BBQ ASPARAGUS

Asparagus is my favourite summer vegetable for grilling. This recipe also works well with bell peppers, sliced onion, zucchini, mushrooms, and eggplant. Serves 4

1 bunch asparagus
⅓ cup olive oil
¼ cup balsamic vinegar
4–5 garlic cloves, crushed

2 Tbsp granulated sugar
1 Tbsp dried basil
kosher salt and freshly ground black
    pepper to taste

Trim off 1 inch of the asparagus from the bottom end of the spears.

In a bowl or shallow pan, whisk together the remaining ingredients to combine. Add the trimmed asparagus and marinate for at least 1 hour at room temperature.

Preheat grill to high.

Lay the asparagus across the hot grill until char marks form, turn to finish the other side, remove, and return to the marinade. Serve immediately.

BBQ CORN IN THE HUSK

This easy barbecue method locks in all the flavour and sweetness that fresh Ontario-grown corn is famous for. It makes for the ultimate corn on the cob experience. Why boil away flavour and valuable nutrients? Try this at least once, and I think you'll be converted for life. Serves 4–8

8 freshly picked ears of corn (Peaches and Cream is my favourite)

Preheat gas grill to medium heat with lid closed for 10 minutes.

Peel back the corn husks, leaving 2 layers, and trim the ends.

Place the corn on the grill and quarter-turn every 5 minutes. The corn should be tender after 20 minutes. Remove from the grill and let rest for 5 minutes before removing the husk. Enjoy as is or try some of the "corndiments" listed below.

Café Confidential: *Corndiments, Anyone?*
- Butter and kosher salt and freshly ground black pepper
- Butter and seasoning salt
- Butter, brown sugar, and salt and pepper
- Butter, chopped garlic, and salt and pepper
- Butter, chopped chives, and salt and pepper
- Butter and chopped tarragon
- Buttertart BBQ Rub (page 107) and butter
- Lime wedges dipped in ground cumin

KILLER FOILED POTATOES

One of the easiest and tastiest ways of cooking potatoes is this no-fuss, wrap-it, heat-it, and leave-it-to-the-barbecue method. The fun is in experimenting with spices and ingredients. Or is the fun in the joy of being outdoors, sitting by the barbecue, and sipping a cold beer? You be the judge. Serves 4

2 large potatoes (I like to use russet
  baking potatoes)
1 small red onion, sliced into rings
¼ cup butter, chilled and chopped
1 tsp paprika

kosher salt and freshly ground black
  pepper to taste
¼–½ cup fresh chopped parsley
1–2 Tbsp Garlic Drizzle (page 56)

Preheat gas grill to medium heat.

Cut the potatoes into ¼-inch slices. Alternately layer potato slices and onion rings on an 18-inch sheet of heavy-duty aluminum foil. Add the butter, paprika, salt, pepper, parsley, and Garlic Drizzle. Cover with another 18-inch sheet of aluminum foil, and fold and seal the edges. Place on the warming upper rack of the grill, away from direct heat, to avoid burning. Cook for 30–40 minutes, or until fork-tender and browned.

Play with your spices a little. Try using oregano, cumin, tarragon, steak spice, basil, lemon juice, or lemon rind. Add little pieces of blue cheese, chives, mushrooms, or zucchini slices. Dare to experiment. Send me your favourite concoction to the contact address listed at www.martysworldfamous.com.

IS THAT POTATO IN MY MASHED GARLIC?

If I had to eat potatoes only one way for the rest of my life, this would be it. Garlicky, creamy, and loaded with flavour, these garlic mashed potatoes always find their way to that comfort zone deep inside my belly. Serves 4

2 lb baking potatoes, peeled and cubed
1½ tsp kosher salt
1 Tbsp olive oil
1 head garlic, peeled

4 Tbsp butter
½ tsp freshly ground black pepper
3–4 Tbsp whipping cream (35%)

In a pot, add the potatoes and ½ tsp of the salt, and cover with cold water. Cover and bring to a boil for 15–20 minutes or until fork-tender.

Meanwhile, heat the olive oil in a small saucepan over low heat. Add all the garlic and slowly brown, 10–15 minutes.

Once the potatoes are tender, drain them then return them to the pot. Add the garlic and oil. Add the butter, the remaining salt, and the pepper, and cream and mash with a potato masher. I prefer a small amount of chunkiness for added texture. This goes great with a Killer Rib Steak (page 117) and grilled vegetables.

For fun, add ½ cup shredded old Canadian cheddar cheese, ¼ cup chopped chives, or ½ cup chopped cooked bacon. Create your own version and enjoy.

Café Confidential: Mealy potatoes—russets, for example—are good for mashing because they contain more dry starch and are denser than waxy potatoes—red-skinned varieties, for example. Cooking swells and separates the cells of the mealy potatoes and creates a lovely fluffy texture.

HORSERADISH SAUCE

This is a smooth sauce with a kick. It's great with Tender Beef Brisket (page 113) or the Men's Night Steak Sandwich (page 114). It also goes great with deli sandwiches. Makes 1 cup

4 tsp granulated sugar
⅛ tsp kosher salt
1 Tbsp white vinegar

1 cup mayonnaise
3 Tbsp prepared horseradish

In a small bowl, dissolve the sugar and salt in the vinegar. In a blender, combine the mayonnaise, horseradish, and vinegar solution. Blend for 15 seconds. Store in the fridge, covered, for 2 hours. Serve.

FISHIN' MUSKOKA

I have heard it said that if you take a child fishing before the age of ten, they're most likely to enjoy the sport later on and throughout their lives. That's what happened to me . . . and the fish tales are aplenty!

TOP 5 MUSKOKA FISHING HOTSPOTS

My all-time favourite leisure activity in Muskoka has to be pickerel fishing. Pickerel is touted as the most delicate, most preferred-tasting freshwater fish in our Canadian Great Lakes system. They're a clever species and catching them is an art. Years of watching the **Bob Izumi's Real Fishing** show have taught me pickerels' feeding habits and how understanding weather conditions can greatly increase your success out on the lake.

BLACK ROCK POINT, LAKE ROSSEAU

My grandfather, Ziggy, and I landed a 24 lb lake trout one August morning around 7:30 am. We were using a white tube jig with a ¾ oz weighted hook. We went with a slow jigging presentation 1–2 feet off the bottom in 60–70 feet of water. Very rarely will you get "skunked" here.

FRANK ISLAND, LAKE MUSKOKA

Fish the Port Carling side of this island in 30–35 feet of water. My favourite technique of jig and minnow landed me a 13 lb blue pickerel through the ice. We had the fish treated by a taxidermist so we could save it for posterity. You can see it on the back wall of the café.

MILLIONAIRE'S ROWE, LAKE MUSKOKA

Just out from the north entrance of Millionaire's Rowe in the middle of the lake are three sunken islands that come up from 120 feet of water into 30 feet. On one magical evening, I landed 6 pickerel, all over 5 lb with the largest being 11 lb, and I finished that off with a 21 lb northern pike slamming my rod as it lay unattended while I was cleaning up to leave. All were caught with my jig and minnow technique while drifting and all were let go. This was one of my most memorable outings.

ELEANOR ISLAND, LAKE MUSKOKA

As you head out of the Muskoka River, turn left and go straight 1 mile toward Gravenhurst. This island is also a bird sanctuary and houses a wide variety of fish species from bass in 4–20 foot depth, walleye at 10–35 foot depth, and lake trout in 35–110 foot depth. A hook and worm will keep the kids busy for hours here in the shallower water.

GOVERNMENT DOCK, WINDERMERE, LAKE ROSSEAU

Just out 100 yards from the government dock in Windermere in 50–60 feet of water—a large number of smaller lake trout migrate here in the winter. Easily accessible by car, this winter ice-fishing hotspot is best from 9 in the morning to 12 noon and 3 to 5 in the afternoon.

#1 BAIT OF CHOICE

I've caught more big fish with this set-up than any others combined.

Warning: If squeamish, turn to the next page.

- ¼ oz lead head jig, long shank, lead colour for a natural silver presentation
- 3–4 inch silver minnow

Take a lively minnow and place the hook cleanly through the mouth and out the side of the gill without piercing the minnow. Turn the minnow upright and push up onto the ball of the jig, opening the minnow's mouth. With forward pressure, slightly lift and bend the minnow and pierce the hook from the belly through to the top dorsal. Avoid hooking the spine or the minnow will die. You'll want it lively to better attract the big fish. The minnow works best when hooked perfectly straight in line with the hook.

HOW TO BRING HOME MORE FISH

When I was younger, I used to get "skunked" after a full day of fishing. Thanks to fishing shows on television and article after article of magazine how-tos and modern technology, the fishing gods have been kinder to me and it's been a whole lotta fun. Here's what's helped me.

Stiff Tip Rods Rule: A stiffer tipped rod or "fast tip" lets you feel more of what's going on beneath the surface. You'll be able to feel the difference between a rock, weeds, hitting the bottom, and a strike. I prefer a good-quality graphite rod like a Shimano 7 foot, medium action, cork handled, fast tipped rod.

Use a Braided or No-Stretch Line: When no-stretch line is combined with a stiff tip rod the sensitivity from the bait to your hand is incredible. It can be almost impossible sometimes to feel a fish biting when using a soft flexible rod.

Anti-Reverse Reel: Use a good quality, anti-reverse spinning reel with a high gear ratio. The more ball bearings in the reel, the better. Anti-reverse immediately stops the bail from reversing when a fish hits. This helps set the hook quicker.

Set Your Drag Properly: Allow enough tension for a fish to run without breaking your line. Always set your drag by pulling the line from the rod tip, not near the spool.

Keep Constant Tension: Avoid slack in your line while fighting a fish. Fish have clever ways of spitting a hook when there is no tension. Believe me, I've lost my fair share.

Give Thanks: Native custom is to practise a blessing when taking fish from the water, sometimes by sprinkling tobacco in the water in thanks. Before I start fishing, I always release one minnow and ask the spirit gods for good luck.

Visualize: See and feel yourself catching the "Big One" and sooner or later it will happen. I learned this from my friend Hap Wilson years ago. Hap is an author, photographer, and artist, and is widely recognized as being our foremost authority on canoe adventure guiding in Canada.

If these tips help land you the big one, please send me a picture to the contact address listed at www .martysworldfamous.com. I'd love to see it.

MY SECRET SMOKED FISH RECIPE

After years of enjoying fishing, I've also gathered proven techniques for smoking fish. There are several varieties of wood chips and different brines to choose from, but this is my go-to recipe for guaranteed best results. You'll need a smoker. Makes 10 fillets • Serves 10

1 cup red wine

1 cup brown sugar, packed

½ cup soy sauce

7 garlic cloves, crushed

2 Tbsp kosher salt

1 Tbsp freshly ground black pepper

12 cups water

10 smaller rainbow trout fillets

alder wood chips

In a large, glass bowl, combine the wine, sugar, soy sauce, garlic, salt, and pepper, and whisk together. Add the water and stir. Submerge the fillets in this marinade. Cover the bowl with plastic wrap and refrigerate for 18–24 hours.

Remove the fish from the marinade and pat dry with paper towel. Place on smoker racks, skin side down, and let air dry for 6–8 hours, until sticky to the touch. This helps the smoke adhere better to the fish.

Soak the alder wood chips in water for 1 hour before smoking the fish. Drain. Submerge the rack of fish into the smoker. Place the wood chips in the pan at the bottom of the smoker. Plug in the smoker and replace the wood chips 3–4 times after they have been scorched and burned up, about every 45–60 minutes. Finish drying without wood chips in the smoker. The total time required is 6–12 hours, depending on your desired doneness. I like smoked fish a little dryer so it has more of a jerky-like texture (12 hours), but a softer, less chewy texture is also fantastic (about 6 hours).

I often serve smoked trout in smaller chunks on crackers and I use this recipe to make my Smoked Trout Pâté (see facing page). It's great for party platters.

SMOKED TROUT PÂTÉ

This simple appetizer is perfect for parties and informal gatherings.
It's super-simple, but it makes a lasting impression. Makes 1 cup

1 cup smoked trout, skin removed (see
    facing page)

2 Tbsp Horseradish Sauce (page 124)

2 tsp tomato paste

1 tsp mayonnaise

1 tsp lemon juice

1 tsp Dijon mustard

kosher salt and freshly ground black
    pepper to taste

Combine all the ingredients in a food processor and blend until smooth. Serve with
crackers or raw vegetables.

Café Confidential: If you're short for time, smoked trout from the supermarket works
just fine for this recipe. I won't tell if you don't!

KILLER MUSSELS

When I make mussels, I like the broth to be so good you want to drink what's left over. This is usually what happens when I serve this recipe to friends and family. Serves 2 as a main course or 4 as an appetizer

3 Tbsp extra virgin olive oil
3 Tbsp butter
1 small onion
7 garlic cloves, minced
1 cup dry white wine
2 lb mussels, scrubbed and beards
    removed

⅓ cup whipping cream (35%)
3 Tbsp chopped fresh basil
kosher salt and freshly ground black
    pepper to taste
2 Tbsp chopped fresh parsley

Heat the olive oil and butter in a large pot over medium-high heat. Add the onion and garlic and cook until soft and golden. Add the wine and bring to a boil. Add the mussels, cover, and cook for 5–7 minutes until the shells open. Discard any shells that don't open. Add the cream, basil, and salt and pepper. Cook for another 2 minutes and stir until it comes to a slight boil. Serve and sprinkle with the parsley to taste.

Add a fresh baguette for dipping and you've got a meal to remember.

CHEF MICHAEL SMITH'S FAVOURITE MARITIME CLAM CHOWDER

The East Coast is one of the greatest regions in Canada. The people are friendly, the scenery is outstanding, and the chowder is exceptional. I'm delighted to have Chef Michael Smith of Prince Edward Island share his recipe with us for your enjoyment. Serves 4 with seconds

"There are many ways to make a traditional clam chowder and just as many stories about its true origins. The best recipes are always the simplest and this is my favourite for chowder. It's the one I make at home. It features classic easy-to-find ingredients; it's a cinch to make and best of all it tastes great!"
—*Chef Michael Smith*

8 slices of bacon, chopped
1 medium cooking onion, chopped
2 celery stalks, diced
1 cup whipping cream (35%)
1 cup milk
½ cup of Chardonnay or other white wine
two 5 oz cans clam meat

1 cup grated baking potato (raw)
2 large bay leaves
1 teaspoon of fresh thyme leaves
one 10 oz can evaporated milk
¼ cup chopped flat leaf parsley
salt and pepper

Brown the bacon until crisp in a thick-bottomed soup pot. Pour off half of the fat. Add the onion and celery with a splash of water and sauté for a few minutes until soft.

Add the cream, milk, white wine, and only the juice from the clams. Reserve the meat. Add the grated potato, bay leaves, and the thyme, and bring the mixture to a slow simmer. Continue simmering for 15 minutes until the grated potato softens and the chowder base thickens.

Add the reserved clam meat, the evaporated milk, and the parsley. Bring back to heat. Taste the chowder and add enough salt and pepper to season it. Serve immediately with your favourite biscuits!

Café Confidential: The chowder can be made a day or two in advance and reheated prior to serving. Its flavour actually benefits from resting overnight.

SHRIMP CHARTREUSE

The most memorable shrimp appetizer I've ever had was at the Chartreuse Restaurant in Kleinburg, Ontario. If you get the chance be sure to take in Kleinburg's annual Binder Twine festival. The main street atmosphere alone, with its cozy old world charm and unique buildings, makes this trip worth the drive. Serves 2 to 4

1 Tbsp olive oil
1 Tbsp butter
2 garlic cloves, minced
8–10 large shrimp, raw
2 Tbsp Chartreuse liqueur

1 Tbsp chopped fresh parsley
kosher salt and freshly ground black
   pepper to taste
1 Tbsp whipping cream (35%)

Heat the olive oil and butter in a saucepan over medium-low heat. Stir in the garlic. Add the shrimp and cook 2–3 minutes. After the first flip of the shrimp, add the Chartreuse liqueur, parsley, and salt and pepper. Cook for 1–2 minutes more until the shrimp is pink. Add the cream and stir until combined. Plate and serve immediately with a fresh baguette.

Café Confidential: Chartreuse liqueur dates back to the 17th century. In 1605 the Order of Chartreuse, an order of French monks, were given an ancient manuscript with the title "An Elixir of Long Life." It took until 1737 for an apothecary at the mother house of the order near Grenoble to actually work his way through the complicated manuscript and create Chartreuse elixir. The recipe for the liqueur is top secret, but we do know that it contains 130 all-natural herbs, plants, and flowers and it's based on the original manuscript.

BBQ WINE AND HERB SALMON

Summery and fresh tasting, this salmon is fantastic on the open grill. Serve with Candied BBQ Asparagus (page 119) and Killer Foiled Potatoes (page 122). This marinade also works well on chicken or pork. Serves 4–6

⅓ cup peanut oil
2–3 Tbsp white wine
1 Tbsp onion powder
1 Tbsp dried parsley
rind of ½ a lemon
rind of ½ a lime
2 tsp granulated sugar
1 tsp garlic powder

1 tsp dried mustard powder
1 tsp kosher salt
1 tsp freshly ground black pepper
¼ tsp paprika
¼ tsp cornstarch
pinch of cayenne pepper
4–6 salmon steaks (6–8 oz each)

In a non-reactive bowl, combine all the ingredients except the salmon and stir thoroughly. Add the salmon steaks and marinate for 1 hour, or 2 hours for a more intense flavour.

Preheat a gas grill to medium heat for 10 minutes, lid closed. Brush the grill with oil to prevent sticking. Cook the salmon steaks for 4 minutes per side, or just until the centre is cooked. Those char marks are full of flavour. Serve immediately.

THE ULTIMATE PICKEREL FRY

Would you like to make the ultimate fish-and-chips dinner at home? Make this recipe and serve it with Ted Reader's Colonel Mustard's Slaw (page 65) and the golden french fries from our Poutine recipe (page 94) for an evening meal you soon won't forget. The crispy pan-fry coating is also great on scallops, shrimp, and calamari, and yes, chicken wings, too. Serves 4

SIMPLE PAN FRY

4 Tbsp butter

2 lb fresh pickerel fillets

kosher salt and freshly ground black pepper to taste

1 cup all-purpose flour

In a large preheated saucepan over medium heat, melt the butter. Moisten the fillets with water, season to taste with the salt and pepper, roll in the flour, shake of any excess, and place in the hot pan. Cook for 3–5 minutes, flip, and repeat just until the middle is cooked and the fish is slightly browned.

CRISPY PAN FRY

1 cup all-purpose flour

3 Tbsp cornmeal or corn flour

4 tsp kosher salt

2 tsp seasoning salt

1 tsp onion powder

1 tsp garlic powder

½ tsp freshly ground black pepper

1½–2 cups peanut oil

2 lb fresh pickerel fillets

In a bowl, combine the flour, cornmeal, salt, seasoning salt, onion powder, garlic powder, and pepper.

Heat the oil in a large saucepan over medium heat, until a drop of water spatters. Moisten the fillets with water and roll in the flour mixture, shake of any excess flour, and carefully place the fish in the hot oil in batches. Brown for about 3–4 minutes per side.

Remove the fish from the oil with a slotted spoon and drain off any excess oil with paper towel.

Serve with Tartar Sauce or Cocktail Sauce (page 142).

THE ULTIMATE PICKEREL FRY (CONTINUED)

TARTAR SAUCE

½ cup sweet green relish

½ cup mayonnaise

squeeze of a lemon wedge

Combine in a small bowl for serving.

COCKTAIL SAUCE

½ cup ketchup

3–4 Tbsp prepared horseradish

Combine in a small bowl for serving.

Café Confidential: For a stronger coating flavour for the fish, add the following to the crispy pan fry recipe:

- 1 Tbsp dried mustard powder
- 1 tsp paprika
- 1 tsp kosher salt
- ½ tsp freshly ground black pepper

Café Confidential: For fun-eating fish sticks the kids will enjoy, cut the fillets into 1-inch strips before coating. Cooking time is 2–4 minutes per side.

TUNA WITH LIME AND CHEDDAR MELT

This recipe was born of necessity. I had run out of sandwich meats after an early lunch rush and scrambled to whip this up as a substitute. It turned out surprisingly well. In fact, it's good enough to be classed as my favourite tuna salad and it's more than worthy of these pages. I hope you like it as much as I do. Makes 4 sandwiches

two 7 oz cans chunk tuna in oil
   or water, drained
1 celery stalk, chopped fine
2 green onions, chopped fine
1 Tbsp Dijon mustard
rind of 1 whole lime
juice of 1 whole lime
2 tsp granulated sugar

½ tsp kosher salt
¼ tsp freshly ground black pepper
8 slices bread, 1 inch thick (I prefer
   cheddar loaf for this recipe)
enough butter for 8 slices of bread
4 slices cheddar cheese
pickles for garnish

In a bowl, combine the tuna, celery, green onions, Dijon mustard, lime rind and juice, sugar, salt, and pepper. Butter 2 slices of bread and place butter side down in a large pan over low heat. Add one-quarter of the tuna mix to each slice of bread and top with a cheddar slice. Butter another 2 slices of bread and place on the tuna with the butter side facing up. When the bottom of the bread is toasty brown, flip, and brown the other side. Cover the pan to help the cheese melt. Remove from the pan, cut on the diagonal, and garnish with pickles. Repeat with the remaining bread and tuna mix.

This goes great with Marty's Red Pepper Soup (page 49) or Opa's Mushroom Soup (page 52).

CASTRO'S PAELLA

During my year in Europe, I spent several months in Nerja, Spain. While there, helping out at Ayo's on La Playa Blanca became a daily ritual. Ayo taught me the art of making paella for 300 people, an inspiring experience. Ayo's is the same restaurant where many of the original Trivial Pursuit questions were written. Being regarded as the best paella maker in the south of Spain, Ayo has been flown to Cuba to cook this dish for Fidel Castro. Here's what Ayo taught me. Serves 8

2 Tbsp olive oil

6 chicken thighs, skin removed, bone in

6 garlic cloves, chopped

½ Spanish onion, diced

½ cup diced red bell pepper

½ cup diced green pepper

2 tsp Spanish paprika

¾ tsp sea salt

½ tsp freshly ground black pepper

1 cup Spanish or Italian risotto rice, rinsed (arborio is ideal)

2 cups chicken stock (page 55)

2 saffron heads, 20 strands

12 large shrimp, raw

12 large scallops

16 fresh mussels, debearded

On medium-high heat, heat a Marty's World Famous Pan or large saucepan. Add the oil to the hot pan. Add the chicken and brown for 10 minutes. Add the garlic and onion, and sauté for 2–3 minutes. Add the peppers, paprika, salt, and pepper and sauté for 3–5 minutes.

Add the rice and stir to combine with the other ingredients. Add the chicken stock and saffron all at once and bring to a boil. Reduce the heat to low, bring the mix to a slow boil, then simmer. Do not stir after you've added the saffron.

After 10–15 minutes at a slow simmer (the rice should be starting to dry but still show some moisture), submerge the shrimp, scallops, and mussels into the rice and remaining liquid.

As the stock evaporates, a slight browning on the bottom will appear. This is ideal.

When the seafood has finished cooking, about 5–8 minutes, and the stock has all been absorbed, remove from heat, and let stand covered with aluminum foil 5 minutes. Stir and serve.

And that's how Castro likes it!

Café Confidential: "Risotto" literally translates as "little rice." You really do need to use arborio rice—named after the town in the Po Valley where it's grown—because its high starch content produces the required creaminess of risotto. Long-grain rice just won't cut it for risotto.

BUTTERTART SECRET REVEALED

"CUT IT, SHAPE IT, FILL IT, AND BAKE IT!"

When Marty's World Famous Café began receiving accolades and praise for winning a **Toronto Star**'s best buttertart competition, I realized that people loved buttertarts from coast to coast to coast and that many people are extremely passionate about these tasty morsels.

BUTTERTART BANTER IS ALWAYS PASSIONATE:

- They've gotta have raisins.
- They can't have raisins.
- They've gotta be runny.
- I like 'em firm.
- Do they have nuts?
- Leave out the walnuts.
- Do they have pecans?
- Do I eat it with a spoon?
- You've gotta eat it with your hands.

The debate over runny versus firm, nuts versus raisins, and corn syrup versus maple syrup will always play a role in defining the perfect buttertart. But the one constant is the *love-energy* that bakers put into their creation. As I researched the origins and history of the buttertart in Canada, I discovered that from coast to coast to coast, every person who loves buttertarts has a story to tell about how their mother, father, grandmother, or grandfather made the best tarts. If passion and love go into the cooking process, the buttertart radiates love. For me, this epitomizes my philosophy of cooking from the zone. The more we create in the kitchen while working from the zone, the better the cook we become, regardless of our skill or training.

Being a loving admirer and consumer of buttertarts, I set out to make a really good buttertart that people would remember and cherish for years to come. In the course of my journey, I discovered many things. The crust should be flaky and melt in your mouth yet be firm enough to carry the filling without leaking. The ratio of filling to pastry requires a fine balance, and the filling should ooze slowly to please both the runny and firm aficionados. Remember that raisin lovers will still eat a plain tart, but you'll have a hard time giving away a raisin tart to a raisin hater. It's just the way it is. So to please the masses, our buttertart crust is made using a century-old nuns' recipe from Quebec combined with my mother's filling, with, of course, a twist.

MARTY'S BUTTERTART KIT

How could I share my buttertart with every Canadian without compromising quality, ingredients, and appearance? Some two years later the answer finally popped into my head. They have to be home-made! What I then discovered was that people thought they were difficult to make. In a way that's true, but that's all about to change.

Pastry breakage can be a real challenge when making buttertarts. There were times at the café when our breakage rate could hit as high as 30 percent. I realized that a hand-held press to form the dough to create a consistent wall thickness would minimize the breakage. This was my *Eureka!* moment. I sketched out my idea on a napkin and later had the press hand-lathed from genuine Canadian maple wood—nothing less would do for my new invention.

The next challenge was to work out how much filling to add to the tart. This led me to add a ring line indicator to the buttertart press. The line indicator indents the pastry without weakening it and leaves a visual fill line for the tart-maker to fill up to. The results were incredible. Consistent, handmade tarts, filled and formed perfectly and easily every time.

It is so easy to do and they're so good to eat. At the time this book went to press, the buttertart kit, including the buttertart press and large buttertart pans, is patent pending. In the meantime, you can see it at www.martysworldfamous.com.

SEARCHING FOR THE PERFECT PASTRY RECIPE

Many people are in search for the perfect crust. They'll sample hundreds and hundreds of pies in a lifetime to fulfill their quest. My mother is one of those people. If she came across a pie crust that didn't satisfy, you heard two things: the fork hitting the plate and the word "nope." Although she may have enjoyed the filling, the pie was always rated by its crust.

After years of searching, Mom finally (and thankfully!) found the perfect pie crust. The in-laws, the Desjardins family from Quebec, had always used a crust recipe from the nuns at La congrégation des Sœurs grises (The Grey Nuns) in Quebec. This century-old recipe is super-flaky with melt-in-your-mouth texture and fantastic flavour.

CENTURY-OLD NUNS' PASTRY DOUGH

We use this pastry for our buttertarts, pies, strudels, and apple dumplings. People often wonder what makes our pastry so flaky and tender. Wonder no more! This is the recipe used by La congrégation des Sœurs grises in Quebec, and was passed on to my family in Montreal, the Desjardins, then to me, and now—with my pleasure—it's being passed on to you. It amazes me how a recipe can survive so long, but there's a simple explanation. Love.

When I'm making the pastry for our buttertarts, I often visualize myself living in a monastery and imagining the peace and tranquility the lifestyle instills. This may seem odd to some but the pastry turns out perfect every time. Coincidence? You decide. Makes 1 head of dough

4 cups all-purpose flour
1 Tbsp kosher salt
rind and juice of ½ a lemon

1 lb lard (we recommend Tenderflake)
1 egg, separated

Sift the flour into a large bowl. Add the salt and lemon rind (reserving the juice), and stir with a whisk. Cut the lard into small cubes. Use a pastry knife to chop the lard and flour together into smaller pea-sized pieces until the mix resembles a light, floury crumble.

Separate the egg white into a bowl for whisking and the yolk into a measuring jug. Add the lemon juice to the egg yolk, top with ice-cold water to the 1-cup line, and stir well.

Whisk the egg white until foamy and white.

Make a well in the flour mixture.

Add the egg yolk, lemon juice, and water mixture to the flour mixture and gently fold 7–12 times by hand. While the mix is still a bit floury, add in the whipped egg white and gently press, fold, and press again until all the flour combines into a paste-like ball.

If you're making buttertarts, divide the dough into 2 balls, wrap with plastic wrap, and chill for 1 hour before using. If you're making 10-inch pie crusts, divide it into 3 before wrapping and chilling. If you're making 1 Big Ass pie, divide two-thirds of the pastry into one ball, and the remaining one-third into another before wrapping and chilling. See also page 159.

If you'd like a visual demonstration, you can watch Marty prepare this recipe at www.martysworldfamous.com.

TIPS FOR PERFECT PASTRY

- Chill the lard in the refrigerator for 1 hour before use. We use Tenderflake for the absolute ultimate flakiness and flavour.
- Sift the flour.
- Use a chilled stainless steel bowl.
- Don't over-cut the lard into the flour, making it sticky; it should be extremely loose and light.
- Use fresh eggs. Stale eggs will not whip properly.
- Whip the egg whites in a clean, steel bowl. Any residue grease, lard, or egg yolk will reduce the fluffiness of the egg white.
- Ice-cold water is best.
- Make a well in the middle of the flour for the egg yolk mixture.

- Fold the flour and egg mixtures together with your fingertips from the outer edges in just until it starts to come together with a touch of dryness remaining. Then add the egg white, and fold and lightly press just until all the flour comes together.
- Wrap and chill the dough in the refrigerator for 1 hour before using.
- Use enough flour for your table and rolling pin. This is more of a paste dough and flour won't dry it out too much at this point.
- Apply even pressure when rolling the dough and slightly lift the rolling pin as you near the edges.
- Be relaxed and enjoy the moment.

IF YOU'RE MAKING PASTRY FOR BUTTERTARTS: GO BIG!

One of the things that makes our buttertarts so fun and unique is the sheer size of them. The simplest and most foolproof way to make a buttertart is to use Marty's Buttertart Kit. (Check them out at www.martysworldfamous.com.) If you don't yet have a kit, I recommend using jumbo muffin pans. Jumbo muffin pans are available at a few kitchen stores and department stores. They have 6 cup-shaped depressions; each is nearly 4 inches in diameter and about 1½ or 2 inches deep. Roll out the pastry until it is about ⅛–¼ inch thick. To cut the pastry to size, use a 6-inch round cookie cutter or anything that is 6 inches in diameter (an empty margarine container is perfect!). Anything smaller just won't cut it!

One head of Century-Old Nuns' Pastry Dough will make enough pastry to fill 3–4 jumbo muffin pans, about 18–22 jumbo buttertarts.

IF YOU'RE MAKING PASTRY FOR PIES: GO BIG ASS!

Likewise, one of the things that makes our pies so unique is their size. If you really want to make a lasting impression, you can buy a Marty's Big Ass Pan (they are available at www.martysworldfamous.com). These pans are no less than 16 inches in diameter and 4 inches deep! One head of Century-Old Nuns' Pastry Dough will make enough pastry for 1 double-crust Big Ass pie, or 1 Big Ass pie with a lattice top. If you are making a single-crust Big Ass pie, you will have one-third of the dough left over. (The single-crust pies in this book are the Big Ass Apple Pie [page 172], Muskoka Maple Pie [page 174], and Real Pumpkin Pie [page 181].) Freeze the leftover dough for later use.

If you don't yet have your Big Ass pan, the pastry recipe will make enough for 3 pie crusts using a deep-dish 10-inch pie plate. This means either 2 pies—1 double-crust pie plus 1 single-crust pie—or 3 single-crust pies. If you wish to make one 10-inch pie, divide the filling amounts listed in the pie recipes by half.

MARTY'S WORLD FAMOUS BUTTERTARTS

Here it is, Canada! The secret recipe that has been safeguarded for years is now yours to enjoy. I would be honoured if you sent me in photos of your friends and family eating these tarts. Please send them to the contact address listed at www.martysworldfamous.com. Makes 18–22 jumbo buttertarts

1 recipe Century-Old Nuns' Pastry Dough (page 154)	6 eggs
	2½ Tbsp vanilla
¾ lb butter, melted	1½ Tbsp fresly squeezed lemon juice
3 cups brown sugar, packed	1½ tsp kosher salt
3 cups corn syrup, slightly warmed in the microwave oven	1½ tsp lemon rind
	⅛–¼ tsp nutmeg (the secret ingredient)

Preheat oven to 375°F and grease 2 jumbo muffin pans or 2 Marty's buttertart pans.

Roll out half the pastry dough until it's about ¼–⅛ inch thick. (Two stacked loonies are the right thickness.) Cut out 6-inch circles of pastry. You will end up with about 18–22 pastry circles after rolling the other half as well as rerolling the pastry scraps. (Don't worry, the rerolled pastry will remain unbelievably tender.) Fill the pans; reserve the remaining circles for the second batch of baking. Set the pastry circles and the pans in the fridge to keep cool while preparing the filling.

In a large bowl with an electric mixer, add the melted butter and sugar, and beat slowly for 2 minutes. Add the remaining ingredients and mix until just combined. Add to the prepared tart shells. If using Marty's Buttertart Kit, fill to the tart press line indicator (or about three-quarters full) and bake for 25–27 minutes. The filling should boil slightly and the crust should look golden.

Cool for 1–2 hours in the pan. Remove with a butter knife, loosening edges and lifting out. Repeat the whole process using the remaining pastry. All that's left now is to sit back and enjoy the compliments. And the tarts, of course!

Café Confidential: *For Raisin Lovers Only*
Add 1 tsp of raisins to the bottom of each tart before you pour in the filling. Pre-soak the raisins in hot water for 15 minutes and strain.

Café Confidential: *If You're Going Nuts*
Add 4–5 pecan halves or 1 Tbsp of crushed walnut pieces per tart.

MARTY'S BUTTERTART SPECIAL

The ultimate dessert at Marty's is this warm, oven-fresh buttertart accompanied by fresh blackberries, vanilla ice cream, and a sprig of mint. Dazzle your company at your next gathering. They'll leave eventually . . . honest. Serves 1

1 oven-fresh buttertart (page 161)
3–4 blackberries
1 scoop vanilla ice cream

1 sprig mint
icing sugar for dusting

On a large plate, arrange the warm buttertart to the side. Add a scoop of fresh vanilla ice cream and arrange the blackberries to please your eye. Finish with a sprig of mint and dust with icing sugar.

Café Confidential: *Make It Your Creation!*
Of course you can substitute the blackberries with raspberries, blueberries, or your favourite fruit or berry.

BIG ASS PIES

My mother called me one day and said, "I've made something for you to try in the store." "What is it?" I asked. "You'll have to wait and see," she replied. To my surprise she had made the largest and tastiest apple pie I had ever seen or tried. People's eyes started to pop out of their heads. We needed a name for this formidable creation . . . and fast. "This is one big ass pie," I said in awe.

The name stuck, and people often bring in their friends and relatives just to gawk and stare at this jaw-dropping, mammoth pie. They're huge: about 14 inches across and 3–4 inches deep. Today we sell thousands of our custom-made, Big Ass pans with our personal logo. You can see them at www.martysworldfamous.com.

MAKING THE PERFECT PIE SHELL

How to make the perfect pie shell? First, start by making the perfect pie pastry dough (page 154). Next, try visualizing your hands gently kneading the dough at a calm and easy pace. Close your eyes. You are rolling a perfect circle with even thickness all the way around. Envision yourself lifting the dough gently into the pan, trimming off the excess, and tucking the edge into a perfect bead along the rim of the pan. Practise this exercise in your mind until you can feel the process. Now you're there. Open your eyes and begin.

Place the dough (page 154) on a floured surface and gently apply a little flour to the top of the dough. With a rolling pin, apply gentle even pressure in all directions, turning the dough if necessary. Roll to an even (¼-inch) thickness. Lifting the pin slightly as you near the outer edge will help create consistent thickness. (See also Tips for Perfect Pastry, page 156.)

Once the dough is large enough to give a 3-inch overhang, gently fold it in half, lift with the rolling pin, and place the fold line halfway across the pan. Unfold the other half of the dough and gently press into the lightly greased pan. Cut away any excess and leave a 2-inch overhang all around. Roll the overhang underneath itself, creating a rolled rim.

Gently flour your hands and crimp or flute the dough between your thumb and index fingers using both hands. You can watch a demonstration at www.martysworldfamous.com. You'll be pleasantly surprised by how straightforward it really is!

PREPARING LATTICE

Roll out about one-third of a head of dough to form an approximate 10- × 18-inch rectangle about ⅛ inch thick. With a sharp knife, cut 1-inch-wide strips 18 inches long. Cover the tops of the pies with 4 strips one way and 3 strips in the opposite direction. Trim off the excess overhang, leaving enough dough to be tucked and re-fluted under the crust at the rim of the pan.

Brush off any excess flour and brush with egg wash.

If you like the braided over-and-under pattern, lay out this design on your work surface. Roll the dough onto your rolling pin, lift, and unroll it onto your pie. Trim, tuck, and re-flute. If you have a little helper in the kitchen, ask him or her to lift the lattice while you braid over and under.

EGG WASH

1 egg yolk
¼ cup 10% cream, 2% milk, or water

I always think a golden brown pie that's been brushed with egg wash looks more appealing and appetizing than one that isn't. Whisk together the yolk and the liquid in a small bowl. Use a dry brush to remove any excess flour from the pastry before applying the egg wash. Try to avoid spilling excess egg wash into your pie, especially with lattice fruit pies.

BIG ASS APPLE PIE

If you really want to have some fun with your friends and family, make this pie. I guarantee that they'll talk about it forever. It is perhaps the biggest slice of pie you'll find anywhere in North America. Makes 1 single-crust Big Ass Pie (see page 159)

CRUST
1 recipe Century-Old Nuns' Pastry
    Dough (page 154)

½ cup melted butter
½ cup raisins (optional)
⅓ cup walnut pieces (optional)

FILLING
5 lb of peeled, cored, and sliced apples
rind and juice of 1 lemon
1 cup brown sugar, packed
½ cup granulated sugar
½ cup all-purpose flour or cornstarch
1 tsp kosher salt
1 tsp cinnamon
¼ tsp nutmeg

CRUMBLE
2 cups whole oats
½ cup brown sugar, packed
3 Tbsp butter
2 Tbsp all-purpose flour
pinch kosher salt
pinch cinnamon

Preheat oven to 375°F.

Prepare a pie shell using two-thirds of the pastry dough. Place the pie shell in a Marty's pan. (Freeze the remaining one-third of the pastry dough for later use.)

For the filling, in a large bowl, combine the filling ingredients and fold until evenly coated. Fill the pie shell.

For the crumble, in another bowl, combine the crumble ingredients and squeeze together in your hands until moistened, and mix until it forms a crumbly mixture. Sprinkle overtop the pie. Bake for 1½ hours or until the sauce bubbles. Cool 1 hour before serving.

Café Confidential: My favourite apples are Northern Spy, Golden Delicious, and Ida Red. Their texture and flavour are ideal for this pie.

MUSKOKA MAPLE PIE

When we introduced this pie to our customers it was an instant hit. After people finish a piece in the café, they often take a piece home for other members of their family. One couple even doubled-back one and a half hours out of their way while on their vacation to pick up another piece. Give it a try. Makes 1 single-crust Big Ass Pie (see page 159)

CRUST
1 recipe Century-Old Nuns' Pastry
   Dough (page 154)

FILLING
6 eggs
2¼ cups pure maple syrup
1½ cups granulated sugar

1½ cups brown sugar, packed
1½ cups 2% milk
1½ cups butter, melted
3 tsp vanilla
3 cups flaked or shredded
   sweetened coconut
2¼ cups rolled oats
1½ cups chopped walnuts

Preheat oven to 375°F.

Prepare a pie shell using two-thirds of the pastry dough. Place the pie shell in a Marty's pan. (Freeze the remaining one-third of the dough for later use.)

In a large bowl, combine the eggs, maple syrup, sugars, milk, butter, and vanilla. Mix in the coconut, oats, and walnuts and pour into the unbaked pie shell. Bake for 60–75 minutes until a cake tester inserted in the centre comes out clean. Cool in the pan.

Serve slightly warm with fresh whipped cream and then sit back and watch what happens. Enjoy.

MUSKOKA BLUEBERRY PIE

Muskoka is known for great quality wild blueberries and thousands of tourists are drawn to the roadside vendors every summer. If you love blueberries, then this pie is a must try. Makes 1 Big Ass Pie (see page 159)

CRUST
1 recipe Century-Old Nuns' Pastry
   Dough (page 154)
egg wash (page 170)

FILLING
8 cups fresh or frozen wild blueberries
three 19 oz cans blueberry pie filling
juice of ½ lemon

Preheat oven to 375°F.

For the crust, roll out two-thirds of the dough to prepare a pie shell. Place the pie shell in a Marty's pan.

For the filling, in a bowl, combine the filling ingredients and fill the pie shell.

Use the remaining one-third of the pastry dough to roll out a top crust. Add the top crust, trim away any excess pastry, and use your finger and thumb to flute both crusts together. Brush with the egg wash. Bake for 1¼ hours or until the top crust is browned.

Remove from the oven and let cool in the pan for 2 hours. Serve with fresh whipped cream or good-quality vanilla ice cream.

MUSKOKA BERRY PIE

Plump blackberries and raspberries come together in this explosion of fruity goodness. As this pie bakes the natural flavours of the berries are released to create just the right amount of sweetness. Another one of my favourites. Enjoy. Makes 1 Big Ass Pie (see page 159)

CRUST
1 recipe Century-Old Nuns' Pastry
    Dough (page 154)
egg wash (page 170)

FILLING
4 cups fresh or frozen raspberries
4 cups fresh or frozen blackberries
three 19 oz cans blueberry pie filling
rind of ½ lemon
juice of 1 lemon

Preheat oven to 375°F.

For the crust, roll out two-thirds of the dough to prepare a pie shell. Place the pie shell in a Marty's pan.

For the filling, in a bowl combine the filling ingredients and fill the pie shell.

Use the remaining one-third of the dough to make a lattice (see page 169) to cover the pie. Leave just enough overhang to tuck and re-crimp the lattice under the rim of the pie shell. Brush the lattice and crust with the egg wash and bake for 1¼ hours or until browned.

Remove from the oven and let cool in the pan for 2 hours before serving.

Good-quality vanilla ice cream is in order here.

Café Confidential: You could replace the raspberries and blackberries with 8 cups mixed berry blend for a taste twist.

BIG ASS CHERRY PIE

Confession time: My willpower deserts me—or is that **desserts** me?—when this pie comes out of the oven. There's something about it that words cannot describe. Makes 1 Big Ass Pie (see page 159)

CRUST
1 recipe Century-Old Nuns' Pastry
    Dough (page 154)
egg wash (page 170)

FILLING
8 cups frozen or fresh, pitted cherries
three 19 oz cans cherry pie filling
rind and juice of 1 lemon
1½ tsp pure almond extract

Preheat oven to 375°F.

For the crust, roll out two-thirds of the dough to prepare a pie shell. Place the pie shell in a Marty's pan.

For the filling, in a bowl, combine the filling ingredients and fill the pie shell.

Use the remaining one-third of the dough to make a lattice (see page 169) to cover the pie. Leave just enough overhang to tuck and re-crimp the lattice under the rim of the pie shell. Brush the lattice and crust with the egg wash and bake in the oven for 1¼ hours or until browned.

Remove from the oven, let cool in the pan for 2 hours, and serve with ice cream.

Café Confidential: My favourite ice cream for this pie is fresh Kawartha Dairy Vanilla Ice Cream. It's the creamiest ice cream I have ever tasted—and I've tasted a lot. This 70-year-old dairy, owned and operated by three generations of the Crowe family, has always valued tradition and quality. At Marty's we always have a huge selection of all their best flavours in stock. Thank you to everyone at Kawartha Dairy. If you make it to Minden or Bobcaygeon, Ontario, stop by and visit the dairy. Just ask a local for directions.

STRAWBERRY RHUBARB PIE

Strawberry fields forever . . . and some rhubarb too. The flavours in this pie are so good I have a hard time putting the fork down . . . after my second piece. Grandma Curtis could really make people smile when she made this pie. Makes 1 Big Ass Pie (see page 159)

CRUST

1 recipe Century-Old Nuns' Pastry Dough
   (page 154)
egg wash (page 170)

FILLING

9 cups fresh or frozen strawberries
7 cups fresh or frozen rhubarb
2½ cups granulated sugar
1¼ cups cold water
juice of 1 lemon
¾ cup cornstarch
½ cup butter

Preheat oven to 375°F.

For the crust, roll out two-thirds of the dough to prepare a pie shell. Place the pie shell in a Marty's pan.

For the filling, in a large pot over high heat, add the strawberries, rhubarb, sugar, ½ cup of the water, and the lemon juice and bring to a boil. Combine the cornstarch with the remaining ¾ cup of water and whisk to combine. Add to the pot and stir. Add the butter. Reduce the heat and simmer for 5 minutes, stirring occasionally. Let cool.

Use the remaining one-third of the dough to make a lattice (see page 169) to cover the pie. Leave just enough overhang to tuck and re-crimp the lattice under the rim of the pie shell. Brush the lattice and crust with the egg wash and bake for 1 hour 20 minutes. Remove and let cool in the pan. Serve slightly warm with good-quality vanilla ice cream.

REAL PUMPKIN PIE

I love when fall rolls around and Thanksgiving comes to my house. The family comes together and I get to make scrumptious pumpkin pie again. This pie is made with fresh pumpkin, real cream, and a unique blend of spices. It's light and fluffy with the odd chunk of pumpkin for added texture. I have to admit—it's really good. Makes 1 single-crust Big Ass Pie (see page 159)

CRUST

1 recipe Century-Old Nuns'
    Pastry Dough (page 154)

FILLING

3–4 small pumpkins (enough to make
    5 cups mashed, cooked pumpkin)
8 eggs

4 cups 10% cream
1¼ cups granulated sugar
¾ cup brown sugar, packed
2½ tsp cinnamon
2½ tsp powdered ginger
1¼ tsp nutmeg
1¼ tsp kosher salt
½ tsp allspice

Preheat oven to 375°F.

Prepare a pie shell using two-thirds of the pastry dough. Place the pie shell in a Marty's pan. (Freeze the remaining one-third of the dough for later use.)

Remove the stems from the pumpkins. Cut each pumpkin in half, remove the seeds, and set them aside to make roasted pumpkin seeds for snacking on (see next page). Cut each half into 3-inch chunks with skin on. Place the chunks skin side down on a baking sheet and bake for 1–1½ hours or until fork-tender. Remove and cool completely. Use a spoon to scoop the flesh into a bowl, and discard the skin. Mash with a potato masher or pulse in a food processor leaving small chunks. You'll need 5 cups of mashed pumpkin for the filling.

In a large bowl or stand mixer, whisk the eggs together. Add the mashed pumpkin and blend. Add the cream, both sugars, cinnamon, ginger, nutmeg, salt, and allspice, gently whisking until well blended.

Add this pumpkin mixture to the prepared pie shell. Bake in the middle of the oven for 1¼ hours, or until the centre is firm. Remove and let cool in the pan for 1–2 hours.

Serve with fresh whipped cream and a pinch of cinnamon. For something different, try crushed peanut brittle on top of the whipped cream. It's fantastic.

(continued on the next page)

REAL PUMPKIN PIE (CONTINUED)

INCREDIBLE PUMPKIN SEEDS

2 cups pumpkin seeds

¼ cup olive oil

1 Tbsp garlic powder

1 tsp sea salt

½ tsp freshly ground
    black pepper

Preheat oven to 400°F.

Wash the pumpkin seeds and pat dry with a paper towel.

In a large bowl, add the seeds, olive oil, garlic powder, sea salt, and pepper.

Pour onto a baking sheet and bake until toasty brown, about 12–16 minutes.

BIG ASS TURKEY PIE

This recipe is a great way to use up any leftover Thanksgiving turkey, bones and all. Deep, rich turkey stock and big chunks of turkey help create the full flavour of this memorable, one-of-a-kind, family pie. Makes 1 Big Ass Pie (see page 159)

CRUST

1 recipe Century-Old Nuns' Pastry
   Dough (page 154)
egg wash of 1 egg yolk mixed
   with 3 Tbsp milk

VEGGIE SWEAT

4 Tbsp butter
1 large onion, chopped
3 large carrots, peeled and sliced
   ¼ inch thick
2 large celery stalks, chopped
¼ tsp kosher salt
¼ tsp fresh ground pepper

FILLING

¼ cup butter
¾ cup all-purpose flour
3 cups turkey stock (see page 55
   for chicken stock and replace
   chicken with turkey)
1 cup 2% milk
1 cup whipping cream (35%)
¼ cup sherry or white wine
juice of ½ a lemon
1 Tbsp chopped fresh thyme
1½ tsp kosher salt
½ tsp fresh ground pepper
⅛–¼ tsp nutmeg
6 cups shredded turkey
1 cup frozen peas

For the crust, roll out two-thirds of the dough to prepare a pie shell. Place the pie shell in a Marty's pan.

For the veggie sweat, in a large saucepan over medium heat, melt the butter. Add the onion, carrots, celery, salt, and pepper and sweat until the carrots soften, about 10 minutes. Set aside. This softens the veggies before the final bake.

To make a roux, melt the butter in a large saucepan over medium-low heat. Slowly whisk in the flour. Whisk in cooled turkey stock until smooth. Add the milk and cream and whisk until smooth. Add the sherry, lemon juice, thyme, salt, pepper, and nutmeg, and stir. Bring to a gentle boil. Add the turkey, the veggie sweat, and the frozen peas and fold to combine. Remove from the heat. Preheat oven to 400°F.

Add the turkey and vegetable mixture to the prepared pie shell. Use the remaining one-third of the dough to make a top crust, cover the pie, and trim any excess dough from the edge. Crimp or flute the top crust to bottom crust. Brush with the egg wash, and cut a hole or pattern in the top of the crust to allow the steam to escape while baking. Bake in the upper half of the oven for 1 hour 20 minutes, or until the centre is bubbling and crust is browned. Serve with a simple salad or soup.

CANADIAN TOURTIÈRE

O Canada! We stand on guard for this! Quebec is probably the province most closely associated with tourtière (meat pie) containing ground pork, spices, and potato, all baked in a melt-in-your-mouth pie shell and served as a Christmas Eve or New Year's Eve tradition. Makes 1 Big Ass Pie (see page 159)

CRUST
1 recipe Century-Old Nuns' Pastry
    Dough (page 154)
egg wash of 1 egg yolk mixed with
    3 Tbsp milk

FILLING
1 Tbsp olive oil
2 large onions, chopped
4 garlic cloves, minced

4 lb ground pork
4 small potatoes, peeled and grated
2 cups beef stock, home-made
    or store-bought
1 Tbsp kosher salt
1 tsp fresh ground black pepper
1 tsp cinnamon
½ tsp allspice
½ tsp ground cloves

For the crust, roll out two-thirds of the dough to prepare a pie shell. Place the pie shell in a Marty's pan.

For the filling, in a large pot over medium heat, add the olive oil, then the onions and garlic. Sauté for 5–10 minutes. Add the pork and potatoes and cook until the meat is no longer pink, about 10 minutes. Add the beef stock, salt, pepper, cinnamon, allspice, and cloves and bring to a boil. Reduce the heat to low and simmer for 1 hour, stirring occasionally. Let cool completely.

Preheat oven to 400°F.

Add the filling to the prepared pie shell. Use the remaining one-third of dough to make a top crust. Cover the filling and use your thumb and finger to trim and flute the pastry. Brush with the egg wash. Cut a hole or pattern in the top of the crust to allow the steam to escape while baking. Bake for 70–80 minutes, until the crust is golden brown.

Serve with My Favourite Simple Salad (page 59) or Opa's Mushroom Soup (page 52).

CHRISTMAS MINCEMEAT PIE

This is another fantastic recipe that people love and come back for year after year during the holiday season. History tells us that this pie was originally made with "minced meat" (beef usually), but it's become common to replace the beef with suet and to put more emphasis on the fruit and spices. A classic holiday flavour for sure that evokes memories of Christmas of old for many people. Makes 1 Big Ass Pie (see page 159)

MINCEMEAT

1 lb sultanas

1 lb currants

1 lb apples, peeled, cored, and
    chopped fine

1 lb beef suet

4½ cups brown sugar, packed

rind and juice of 2 oranges

rind and juice of 2 lemons

¾ cup brandy (optional, but
    recommended)

⅓ lb almonds, chopped fine

1 tsp allspice

½ tsp cinnamon

¼ tsp nutmeg

CRUST

1 recipe Century-Old Nuns' Pastry Dough
    (page 154)

egg wash (page 170)

For the mincemeat, you have two preparation methods:

UNCOOKED METHOD:

In a large bowl, combine all the mincemeat ingredients and mix well. Store in an airtight container and refrigerate for 4–6 weeks. Every 2 weeks fold and stir, then return to the refrigerator until ready to use.

COOKED METHOD:

Reserve half the brandy, if using, and set aside.

In a large pot over low heat, combine all ingredients, including only half the brandy, and simmer, slightly covered, for 1½–2 hours, stirring occasionally. Remove from the heat and stir in the remaining brandy. Let cool completely before using.

(continued on the next page)

CHRISTMAS MINCEMEAT PIE (CONTINUED)

Preheat oven to 400°F.

For the crust, roll out two-thirds of the dough to prepare a pie shell. Place the pie shell in a Marty's pan.

Fill the pie shell with the prepared mincemeat and use the remaining third of the pastry dough to make a top crust or 1-inch lattice design (see page 169), whichever you prefer. Cut a steam vent or circle in the centre if using a top crust. Brush with the egg wash and bake for 1–1¼ hours. Let cool in the pan before serving.

Café Confidential: *Uncooked versus Cooked Mincemeat*
We use the uncooked method at the café to produce a more textured mincemeat. The cooked method produces a softer pie filling with a smoother feel. Either way, you can't go wrong.

Café Confidential: *Preserving Mincemeat with the Cooked Method*
While the mincemeat is still warm, fill sterilized rubber-seal jars with the mincemeat, tighten the lids securely, and store in a cool dry place for up to 1 year. (Did someone say "Christmas in July"?)

SWEET CAFÉ FAVOURITES

Great coffee and tea deserves a mate, and we definitely have a match here with these recipes. These recipes continue to make people smile, so it's only fitting to include them for you to try on your friends and family.

MARTY'S CHOCOLATE CHIP COOKIES

We've sold literally tens of thousands of these buttery, slightly crunchy, slightly chewy cookies. They rank right up there with our buttertarts, muffins, and biscotti as one of our best sellers. They even made the cover of the **Cottage Times**. They're easy to make, so the kids can have fun helping with this creation. They make a great gift at Christmas or a birthday celebration. Give 'em a try. Makes 2 dozen cookies

1 cup butter, softened
1 cup granulated sugar
1 cup brown sugar, packed
2 eggs
1 tsp vanilla
2 cups all-purpose flour

2½ cups whole oats
1 tsp baking powder
1 tsp baking soda
½ tsp kosher salt
1 cup semi-sweet chocolate chips

Preheat oven to 350°F. Grease a cookie sheet.

In a stand mixer or large bowl with an electric mixer, whisk the butter and sugars until light and fluffy, about 3 minutes. Add the eggs and vanilla, and mix until combined.

While still mixing, slowly add the flour until blended.

In a food processor or blender, powder the whole oats, baking powder, baking soda, and salt. Add to the dough mixture and mix until just combined. Fold in the chocolate chips.

Shape the dough into 3-inch puck shaped pieces and bake for 10–12 minutes, or until the edges are slightly browned. Cool on a tray.

Café Confidential: *Two Is Better Than One*
For a twist, put vanilla ice cream between 2 cookies for the ultimate ice cream sandwich.

OUR BEST OATMEAL RAISIN COOKIE

Some cookies are just classics. They're soft, chewy, and packed with flavour. Only chocolate chip can beat these in a popularity contest at Marty's. Makes 2 dozen cookies

3½ cups quick-cooking oats

1¼ cups all-purpose flour

1 cup walnuts or pecans, pieces

1 tsp baking soda

1 tsp kosher salt

½ tsp cinnamon

1 cup shortening (I use Golden Crisco)

1½ cups brown sugar, packed

1 egg

¼ cup warm milk

2 tsp vanilla

1½ cups raisins

Preheat oven to 375°F. Line a cookie sheet with parchment paper.

In a food processor add 1½ cups of the oats, flour, walnuts, baking soda, salt, and cinnamon. Blend or pulse until all ingredients turn into powder, 1–2 minutes.

In a stand mixer with paddle attachment, or using a bowl and electric mixer, cream together the shortening and brown sugar until fluffy, 2 minutes. Add the egg, milk, and vanilla and blend for 1–2 minutes.

Slowly add the prepared dry ingredients on low speed and mix until just combined. Add the remaining oats and the raisins and mix until just combined.

Drop the dough by heaping tablespoons onto the prepared cookie sheet, about 2–3 inches apart.

Bake in the middle of the oven for 10–12 minutes, or just until the edges brown. Cool in the pan. Get out the milk!

GRANNY'S BEST PEANUT BUTTER COOKIES

Granny Curtis could cook. Man, could she cook! My memories of visits to Granny's house as a young boy are filled with freshly baked pies, home-made cookies, and turkey dinners with cranberry sauce, turnips, and mashed potatoes. But one recipe always prevailed. In a blue tin on the counter, or sometimes in a large clear jar, there rested her peanut butter cookies. No mistake about it, the fork-pressed pattern on top gave them away every time. And then there was none. Makes 12 cookies

½ cup butter
½ cup granulated sugar
½ cup brown sugar, packed
1 egg

½ cup smooth peanut butter
1½ cups all-purpose flour
1 tsp baking soda

Preheat oven to 350°F. Grease a cookie sheet.

In a medium-sized bowl, use an electric mixer or stand mixer on medium speed to cream together the butter and sugars. Add the egg and mix well. Add the peanut butter and mix well. Add the flour and baking soda and mix until just combined.

Measure out 1 heaping tablespoonful of dough and form into a ball, pressing gently with the back of a fork. Place on the prepared cookie sheet.

Bake for 10–12 minutes, or until the edges are slightly brown.

Café Confidential: Reduced-fat peanut butter will make the cookie run due to a higher oil content than regular peanut butter. It's all or nothing for this recipe.

CHOCOLAVA

This incredible recipe comes from Julie van Rosendaal of One Smart Cookie fame in Calgary, Alberta. These rich, chocolatey, brownie-like cookies are rolled in icing sugar before they're baked to create a crackled surface as they rise and spread in the oven. When Julie had her bakery, these cookies were her best seller, and generated requests from all over North America. Try them. They're easy—just the way we like it! Makes 2 dozen

1⅓ cups all-purpose flour
1 cup granulated sugar
⅓ cup brown sugar, packed
½ cup cocoa
1 tsp baking powder
¼ tsp salt

¼ cup butter or non-hydrogenated margarine, softened
3 large egg whites or 2 large eggs, lightly beaten
2 tsp vanilla
icing sugar, for rolling

Preheat oven to 350°F. Spray a cookie sheet with non-stick spray.

In a large bowl or in the bowl of a food processor, combine the flour, both sugars, cocoa, baking powder, and salt, being careful to break up any lumps in the brown sugar. Add the butter and pulse, if using a food processor, or stir with a fork or pastry cutter, or whisk until the mixture is well combined and crumbly.

Add the eggs and vanilla and stir by hand until the dough just comes together. Be careful not to overmix. The dough will be fairly dry—it will seem at first that there isn't enough moisture, but if you keep stirring, or get in there and use your fingers, eventually it will come together.

Place a few heaping spoonfuls of icing sugar into a shallow dish. Roll the dough into 1½-inch balls then roll the balls in the icing sugar to coat. Place them about 2 inches apart on the prepared cookie sheet. Bake for 12–14 minutes, until just set around the edges but still soft in the middle. Transfer to a wire rack to cool.

MARTY'S CHRISTMAS SHORTBREAD

What's a festive season without the melt-in-your-mouth, buttery sensation only a shortbread cookie can provide? These cookies really are simple to make before Christmas and you can freeze them ahead of time. The aroma of butter–baked shortbread will put any family in the Christmas spirit. Try drizzling them with melted Belgian chocolate for some variation. Happy Holidays! Makes about 2 dozen cookies

1 cup all-purpose flour
½ cup cornstarch

½ cup icing sugar
¾ cup unsalted butter, softened

Preheat oven to 300°F.

Sift together the flour, cornstarch, and icing sugar in a bowl, then blend in the butter with a wooden spoon until a smooth dough forms.

You now have two options.

FOR SHORTBREAD DROP COOKIES:

While the dough is freshly formed, drop a tablespoonful of dough onto an ungreased cookie sheet and press lightly with a floured fork. Top with a whole pecan or almond or a candied cherry, and bake for 8–12 minutes or until edges are slightly browned.

FOR SHAPE-CUT DESIGNS:

Chill the dough in plastic wrap for up to 1 hour. Roll out ¼ inch thick and cut into the desired shape with a cookie cutter.

Place on a lightly greased baking sheet and bake for 10–15 minutes, or until the edges brown slightly.

Café Confidential: Melt dark Belgian chocolate wafers in the microwave oven, stirring every 30 seconds until completely melted. Use a teaspoon to drizzle in a back and forth motion. Drizzle in the other direction with white Belgian chocolate. You can also completely dip the cookies or dip only one end. You choose! Let cool on waxed paper before devouring.

BELGIAN WHITE CHOCOLATE AND MACADAMIA NUT COOKIES

This is one of our best-selling cookies at Christmas. The combination of rich, white Belgian chocolate and macadamia nuts creates a unique flavour. Decadent to say the least, and yet simple to make. Their slightly crunchy outer edge and softer-textured centre make these cookies difficult to resist. These cookies freeze well if you want a head start on your holiday baking.

Makes about 2 dozen cookies

1 cup whole oats

1 cup all-purpose flour

½ cup pecans, pieces

½ tsp baking powder

½ tsp baking soda

¼ tsp kosher salt

½ cup unsalted butter

½ cup granulated sugar

½ cup brown sugar, packed

1 egg

1½ tsp vanilla

1¾ cups Belgian white
   chocolate chunks

1 cup macadamia nuts, pieces

Preheat oven to 375°F. Line a cookie sheet with parchment paper.

In a food processor, pulse to combine the whole oats, flour, pecans, baking powder, baking soda, and salt, and set aside.

In a bowl, cream the butter and sugars together. Add the egg and vanilla and mix to combine. Stir in the oat and flour mixture until combined. Add the white chocolate and macadamia nuts and combine.

Drop by heaping tablespoons, about 2 Tbsp, onto the prepared cookie sheet, 2–3 inches apart. Bake for 10–12 minutes, or until edges brown slightly. Remove from the pan and transfer to a wire rack to cool.

Café Confidential: If you plan to freeze cookies, make sure they're completely cool before transferring them to the freezer; they'll keep for 3–6 months. It's a good idea to put waxed paper between layers of cookies to stop them from sticking together. Remember to label the storage bag or container clearly, especially if you've frozen a few different types of cookie. Avoid freezing the cookies with frosting on them. Defrost them completely, then add the frosting as normal.

GREEK CRESCENT COOKIES

These sugar-powdered classics are another best seller at our store during the holiday season. The entire recipe is created in a food processor. What could be easier? Try them. Makes about 2 dozen cookies

1 cup icing sugar
¾ cup whole blanched almonds
1 tsp orange rind
1 cup unsalted butter, softened
1 egg yolk
¼ cup brandy

2 Tbsp freshly squeezed orange juice
¼ tsp almond extract
1¾ cups all-purpose flour
½ cup cake and pastry flour
½ tsp baking powder
icing sugar, for rolling

Preheat oven to 350°F. Lightly grease a cookie sheet, or line with parchment paper.

In a food processor, blend the icing sugar, almonds, and orange rind until powdery. Add the remaining ingredients. Pulse just until dough comes together.

Lightly dust the dough with flour; wrap it in plastic wrap and chill for half an hour if the dough is too soft to work with.

Roll the dough into 3-inch ropes, about the thickness of your index finger. Shape them like a smiley face or crescent. Pinch and taper the ends.

Place on the prepared cookie sheet and bake 8–12 minutes, or until the edges just start to turn light brown. Cool for 3–5 minutes on the pan, and while still warm roll in a bowl filled with icing sugar.

Store in an airtight container for up to 1 month. These cookies also freeze extremely well, so they can be made ahead of time for holiday gatherings. After defrosting, you should re-roll or dust them in icing sugar for the ultimate presentation.

Sometimes we drizzle these with dark Belgian chocolate or dip one end in dark chocolate, cool, and cross drizzle with white Belgian chocolate instead of sprinkling them with icing sugar. It creates an entirely new look and flavour.

LEMON, CRANBERRY, AND ALMOND BISCOTTI

There has only ever been one biscotti recipe at Marty's. This flavour combination goes well with all our specialty coffees and large selection of loose-leaf teas. Makes about 2 dozen biscotti

1 cup butter, softened

2 cups granulated sugar

6 eggs

1–2 Tbsp lemon rind (rind of
   1 whole lemon)

1 Tbsp vanilla

5½ cups all-purpose flour

1 Tbsp baking powder

½ tsp kosher salt

¾ cup cranberries, dried

¾ cup sliced almonds

1 cup icing sugar

¼ cup lemon juice

Preheat oven to 350°F. Grease and flour a cookie sheet.

Using a stand mixer or large bowl with electric mixer, cream together the butter and sugar until light and fluffy, about 3 minutes. Add the eggs one at a time, blending well after each addition. Add the lemon rind and vanilla and blend. Combine the flour, baking powder, and salt in a separate bowl and slowly add to the butter mixture just until blended. Add the cranberries and almonds. Blend until evenly distributed.

On a lightly floured surface, roll dough into 2 equal-sized logs. Place on the prepared cookie sheet and shape into 2 parallelograms, about 1 inch thick. Angle both ends of each log on a 45-degree angle. This prevents waste when cutting on an angle. A table scraper will help to shape them.

Bake for 35–40 minutes or until the edges brown slightly and the centre bounces back to the touch. Cool the cookies completely in the pan, then cut into ¾-inch slices on the same angle as the ends. Return the slices to the trays, laying them flat, and bake for a further 10 minutes. (We prefer our biscotti a little softer than most biscotti. For firmer biscotti, flip and bake another 10 minutes at 350°F.)

Let cool completely in the pan. In a bowl, whisk together the icing sugar and lemon juice. Thin out with a touch of hot water if necessary. Drizzle over the biscotti and let the glaze dry. Store in an airtight jar for up to 2 weeks or freeze.

We often bag these in clear Cellophane wrap and tie ribbon at one end. They make great gifts for any occasion.

Café Confidential: If you want larger biscotti, make 1 large log instead of 2, and increase the width. The baking time remains the same. At the café we multiply this recipe by 4 and bake on large 18- × 24-inch baking sheets, which allows us to make biscotti 12–14 inches long. People are in shock when they see them.

MATRIMONIAL CAKE (DATE SQUARES)

We sell thousands of these tasty squares every summer. Soft, chewy, and packed with toasted oat and butter flavour, is it any wonder these treats were commonly served as wedding cake a generation or two ago? Makes one 9- × 13-inch cake

BASE AND CRUMBLE TOPPING	FILLING
1 cup butter	3 cups pitted dates
1 cup brown sugar, packed	1½ cups water
1¾ cups all-purpose flour	1 cup brown sugar, packed
½ tsp kosher salt	¼ cup orange juice
½ tsp baking soda	1 tbsp orange rind
1½ cups whole oats	1 tsp vanilla

Preheat oven to 400°F. Grease a 9- × 13-inch pan.

For the base, in a bowl, cream together the butter and sugar. Add the flour, salt, and baking soda, and mix until just combined. Add the oats, and mix to form a coarse crumble. Set aside.

For the filling, in a pot over high heat, add the dates, water, and sugar, and bring to a boil. Reduce the heat and simmer, covered, for 10 minutes. Mash the dates with a potato masher for a thick, chunky texture. Add orange juice, orange rind, and vanilla, and stir.

Pack half the crumble mixture into the bottom of the pan. Top with the date mixture and finish by sprinkling the remaining crumble mixture lightly overtop. Bake for 25–30 minutes, or until the surface browns nicely. Let cool in the pan. Cut into squares and renew your vows.

Café Confidential: These tasty date squares were once popular as wedding cake in the Prairies, and are still a staple at wedding showers. One explanation I've heard—and was greatly amused by— is that the three textures (solid base with a smooth filling and rough top) represent marriage and all its complexities. Personally, I like to think that the sweetness represents the love.

NANAIMO BARS

Legend has it that a local housewife created these no-bake squares for a magazine cooking contest, and named them after her city: Nanaimo, British Columbia. She won first prize and put her city on the map for all the best reasons. The bars are now known across North America. Thank you to the city of Nanaimo and to the lady who made it happen. Makes one 8- × 8-inch pan

BOTTOM LAYER
½ cup unsalted butter
¼ cup granulated sugar
5 Tbsp cocoa powder
1 egg, beaten
1¼ cups graham wafer crumbs
1 cup shredded sweetened coconut
½ cup finely chopped almonds

MIDDLE LAYER
2 cups icing sugar
½ cup unsalted butter
3 Tbsp 10% cream
2 Tbsp vanilla custard powder

TOP LAYER
4 oz semi-sweet chocolate
2 Tbsp unsalted butter

For the bottom layer, in a double boiler, melt butter, sugar, and cocoa. Add the egg and stir to thicken. Remove from heat and add the graham crumbs, coconut, and almonds. Press into the bottom of an ungreased 8- × 8-inch pan.

For the middle layer, in a bowl, cream together the icing sugar, butter, cream, and vanilla custard powder. Beat until light and fluffy, and spread over the bottom layer.

For the top layer, in a saucepan over low heat, melt the chocolate and butter and pour over the middle layer.

Chill in the refrigerator for 1–2 hours. Cut and serve.

MARTY'S BEST BROWNIES

Rich, chocolatey, and delicious with a toasted nutty twist is the best way to describe these winning brownies, which always sell out at our store. Bring on the milk. Makes sixteen 2-inch squares

8 oz semi-sweet chocolate

¼ cup butter, softened

1 cup walnuts, pieces

1 tsp peanut oil

½ tsp kosher salt

1 cup dark brown sugar, packed

1 tsp pure vanilla

2 large eggs, room temperature

½ cup all-purpose flour

1 tsp baking powder

Preheat oven to 350°F. Grease and flour an 8- × 8-inch pan.

In a large heavy-bottomed saucepan, on the lowest heat, melt the chocolate and butter, stirring constantly until melted. Set aside to cool.

In a small bowl, toss or roll the walnuts, peanut oil, and salt together and bake on a cookie sheet for 4 minutes or just until toasted. Set aside.

Add the brown sugar and vanilla to the chocolate and mix with a wooden spoon to combine. Add the eggs one at a time, mixing well after each addition.

In a separate bowl, mix together the flour and baking powder, add to the saucepan, and mix well. Stir in the baked nuts.

Pour into the prepared pan and bake for 30–35 minutes, or just until the centre is almost firm to the touch and a toothpick inserted into the centre comes out clean.

Let cool in the pan, cut, and serve.

Café Confidential: *Brownie Bowl Supreme*
Place 3 brownies in a bowl and heat them in a microwave oven for 45 seconds. Add fresh vanilla ice cream and chocolate sauce with whipped cream and chocolate shavings. Yum!

PEAR AND WALNUT STREUSEL COFFEE CAKE

Our customers have expressed a particular fondness for this cake. It always sells out fast. Cinnamon, pears, and a walnut butter crumble create a perfect balance with the sour cream flavour. I recommend you try it at least once. Makes one 10-inch cake

NUT MIXTURE
2 cups walnuts, pieces
⅔ cup brown sugar, packed
2 tsp cinnamon

CRUMBLE TOPPING
½ cup butter, cool and chopped
⅔ cup all-purpose flour

FILLING
2 pears
2 tsp lemon juice

FLOUR MIXTURE
3½ cups all-purpose flour
1½ tsp baking powder
1 tsp baking soda
½ tsp kosher salt

BASE
1 cup butter, softened
2 cups granulated sugar
1 Tbsp vanilla
4 eggs
one 16 oz container sour cream

Preheat oven to 400°F. Grease and flour a 10-inch Bundt pan.

For the nut mixture, in a bowl combine the walnuts, sugar, and cinnamon. Set aside.

For the crumble topping, in another bowl, cut the butter into the flour to make a coarse crumble. Stir in 1½ cups of the reserved nut mixture. Set aside.

For the filling, peel, core, and thinly slice the pears. Toss with the lemon juice to prevent from browning. Set aside.

For the flour mixture, in a clean bowl, combine the flour, baking powder, baking soda, and salt. Set aside.

For the base, in a large stand mixer with paddle attachment, or large bowl and electric hand mixer, on medium speed, cream together the butter, granulated sugar, and vanilla. Add the eggs one at a time, mixing well after each addition until blended. Add the reserved flour mixture and the sour cream alternately on low speed just until blended.

Pour two-thirds of the cake batter into the prepared bundt pan. Sprinkle the remaining nut mixture over the batter, layer on the sliced pears, cover with the remaining batter, and top with the crumble mixture. Bake between 1–1½ hours in the upper half of your oven, or until a cake tester inserted in the centre comes out clean. Cool in the pan. Remove and serve slightly warm with real whipped cream.

INGEBORG'S CARROT CAKE

My mother's sister, Inge, loves to bake and she is regarded as one of the better bakers in the family when it comes to cakes, muffins, and loaves. The buttermilk glaze on this cake is the key to its moisture and added flavour, and the frosting speaks for itself. This will be a huge hit with whomever you serve this to. Guaranteed. Thanks, Inge. Serves 8–12

CARROT CAKE

2 cups all-purpose flour

2 tsp baking soda

2 tsp cinnamon

½ tsp kosher salt

3 eggs

2 cups granulated sugar

¾ cup vegetable oil

¾ cup buttermilk

2 tsp vanilla

one 8 oz can pineapple, drained
    and crushed

2 cups grated carrots

1¼ cups shredded sweetened coconut

1 cup coarsely chopped walnuts

BUTTERMILK GLAZE

1 cup granulated sugar

½ cup buttermilk

½ cup butter

1 Tbsp corn syrup

½ tsp baking soda

1 tsp vanilla

CREAM CHEESE FROSTING

½ cup butter, softened

one 8 oz package cream cheese, softened

1 tsp vanilla

2 cups icing sugar

1 tsp orange juice

1 tsp orange rind

(continued on page 208)

INGEBORG'S CARROT CAKE (CONTINUED)

Preheat oven to 350°F. Generously grease two 9-inch round cake pans.

For the cake, in a bowl sift together the flour, baking soda, cinnamon, and salt, and set aside.

In another large bowl beat the eggs, then add the sugar, oil, buttermilk, and vanilla, and mix well. Add the flour mixture, pineapple, carrots, coconut, and walnuts and stir well with a spatula.

Divide the mixture evenly between the 2 prepared pans and bake for 55 minutes, or until a toothpick inserted in the centre comes out clean.

While the cakes are baking, prepare the glaze. In a saucepan on the stovetop, combine the sugar, buttermilk, butter, corn syrup, and baking soda, and bring to a boil. Reduce the heat to low, add the vanilla, stir, and simmer for 5 minutes, stirring again. The glaze will turn a brownish colour.

Brush the glaze over the cakes, hot from the oven, until absorbed. Let the cakes cool in the pans on a rack.

For the frosting, whip together the butter, cream cheese, and vanilla. Add the icing sugar and continue whipping. Add the orange juice and rind and whip until well combined.

To assemble the cake, place one 9-inch round on a cake plate. Cover with one-third of the cream cheese frosting, and the second 9-inch round. Cover the top and sides with the remaining frosting. Chill for 1 hour before serving.

MARTY'S CHOCOLATE MALT

This retro drink is a huge hit in the summer at Marty's. I've always loved the 1950s, with the funky cars, the sock hops, the clothing and hairdos, and yes, the food. This shake will take you down memory lane to the malt shops of old. Serves 2

3 scoops chocolate ice cream
½ cup 10% cream
½ cup 2% milk

1–2 Tbsp malt powder (Horlicks is
    good for this)
1–2 Tbsp chocolate syrup

Combine all the ingredients in a blender. Thicker is better for this one. You can also make it with vanilla ice cream. Just increase the chocolate sauce to taste. Enjoy.

MARTY'S CHEESECAKE

A good cheesecake is essential if you run a café that serves quality coffee and espresso-based drinks. This cheesecake perfectly combines a dense, thick-textured filling with a hint of lemon and an incredible short dough crust. You'll be happy you tried this recipe. And you'll be looking for an excuse to try it again. Makes one 10-inch cheesecake

CRUST

2¼ cups all-purpose flour, sifted
⅓ cup granulated sugar
1½ tsp lemon rind
¾ cup butter, softened
3 egg yolks
1 egg white, reserved (for brushing the inside of crust)

FILLING

three 8 oz packages cream cheese, softened
1¼ cups granulated sugar
6 eggs separated
2 cups sour cream
⅓ cup all-purpose flour
2 tsp vanilla
juice of ½ lemon
pinch of nutmeg

Preheat oven to 400°F. Grease a 10-inch springform pan.

For the crust, in a medium bowl combine the flour, sugar, and lemon rind. Work the butter and egg yolks into the flour with your fingertips until you form a smooth dough. Wrap and chill the dough for 30 minutes.

On a lightly floured surface, roll out half the dough to a 10-inch circle and use it to line the bottom of the pan. Prick the dough with a fork. Bake for 15 minutes or until golden brown. Cool in the pan.

Reduce oven heat to 350°F.

Press the remaining pastry along the sides of the pan, 1½–2 inches up from the bottom crust. Brush beaten egg white along the inside bottom crust and sides to seal.

For the filling, in a large bowl with an electric mixer at low speed, beat the cream cheese until soft. Then add the sugar slowly, until fluffy. Beat in the egg yolks one at a time, beating well after each addition. Beat in the sour cream, flour, vanilla, and lemon juice until smooth.

In a large bowl with an electric mixer on high speed, beat the egg whites until stiff peaks form and hold their shape. Fold the egg whites into the cheese mixture until well combined and pour overtop the pastry.

Bake for 1 hour 15 minutes, or until the top is golden. Turn off the oven and allow the cake to cool in the oven for 1 hour. Remove from the oven and cool at room temperature in the pan.

Café Confidential: *Tips for Making Cheesecake*
- If using a convection oven, watch the surface as not to burn the top. Alternatively, turn off the convection.
- Top with your favourite topping. Pie filling works well. Try cherry or blueberry.
- For a fresh berry topping, bring 1 cup of water and 1 cup of granulated sugar to a boil. Cook for 3–5 minutes and stir. Add 1 Tbsp of cornstarch dissolved in ¼ cup of water, and stir. Add 1 cup of your favourite fresh berries and stir gently for 1 minute. Pour a couple of tablespoons over each cheesecake slice. This can be served cool or warm.

Café Confidential: Don't tell her I told you, but my mother once accidentally baked an entire cheesecake thinking that the clear bag of bulk salt was sugar. The moral of the story: label, label, label.

MUSKOKA MAPLE FUDGE

Smooth and creamy with that unmistakable maple flavour. Need I say more?
Makes one 8-inch square pan

2 cups maple syrup   2 Tbsp butter
¾ cup 10% cream

Grease an 8-inch square pan.

In a saucepan over high heat bring all the ingredients to a boil. Do not cover. Using a candy thermometer to monitor the temperature, bring the mix to between 235°F and 240°F then drop a little in cold water. It will form a soft ball when ready. Remove from the heat and monitor the temperature until it drops to 110°F. Beat until creamy.

Pour the fudge into the prepared pan and cool. Cut into squares.

Café Confidential: Try adding ¼ cup chopped walnuts when creaming the fudge.

APPLE PHYLLO TARTS

These are a twist on our Big Ass Apple Pie (page 172), and they can be easily baked in a regular tart pan. When we make these at Marty's they're gone almost the moment they come out of the oven. Makes 12 tarts

THE FILLING
2½ lb apples, peeled, cored, and
   thinly sliced (try Northern Spy
   or Ida Red apples)
⅔ cup brown sugar, packed
rind and juice of ½ lemon
⅓ cup raisins
¼ cup walnut pieces
¼ cup all-purpose flour
¼ cup butter, melted
½ tsp kosher salt
½ tsp cinnamon
¼ tsp nutmeg

PHYLLO
12 sheets phyllo pastry
¼ cup butter, melted

CRUMBLE TOPPING
2 cups whole oats
⅓ cup brown sugar, packed
2 Tbsp all-purpose flour
1½ Tbsp butter, melted

Preheat oven to 375°F. Grease 2 Marty's Buttertart Pans (see page 150) or jumbo muffin pans (see page 159).

For the filling, in a bowl combine all the filling ingredients and toss until evenly coated.

For the phyllo, unwrap the phyllo sheets and layer 2 at a time. Brush with the melted butter every 2 layers. After 6 sheets have been layered, cut into 6 equal rectangles. Do not butter the top layer. Place the phyllo rectangles over the prepared pans. Apply pressure using your Marty's Buttertart Press (see page 150) or gently press the phyllo into the cups.

For the crumble topping, in a bowl, whisk together the oats, brown sugar, and flour. Add the butter and use your hands to press and form into a moist crumble mix.

Divide the apple mix into the phyllo rectangles and top with crumble. Bake for 30–35 minutes. The phyllo will brown nicely and the apple filling will caramelize and bubble. Cool for 15 minutes in the pan, remove, sprinkle with icing sugar, and serve with fresh vanilla ice cream. Add a few fresh berries, and watch the magic happen.

METRIC CONVERSION CHARTS

IMPERIAL	METRIC
¼ tsp	1 mL
½ tsp	2 mL
1 tsp	5 mL
2 tsp	10 mL
1 Tbsp	15 mL
2 Tbsp	30 mL
¼ cup	60 mL
⅓ cup	80 mL
½ cup	125 mL
⅔ cup	160 mL
¾ cup	185 mL
1 cup	250 mL

FAHRENHEIT	CELSIUS
175	80
200	95
225	110
250	120
275	140
300	150
325	160
350	180
375	190
400	200
425	220
450	230

Thankyou Marty

Thanks for the Yummy butter ta[r]...

awesome Coffee Marty!

Jane...
Tori...
+ 5k...

Awe...
Foo...
Pl...

INDEX